Labor Standards
in the
United States and Canada

Labor Standards
in the
United States and Canada

Richard N. Block
Karen Roberts
and
R. Oliver Clarke
Michigan State University

2003

W.E. Upjohn Institute for Employment Research
Kalamazoo, Michigan

Library of Congress Cataloging-in-Publication Data

Block, Richard N.
 Labor standards in the United States and Canada / Richard N. Block,
Karen Roberts and R. Oliver Clarke.
   p. cm.
Includes bibliographical references and index.
  ISBN 0–88099–235–2 (pbk. : alk. paper)—ISBN 0–88099–236–0
(hardcover : alk. paper)
   1. Labor Policy—United States. 2. Labor laws and legislation—United
States. 3. Labor policy—Canada. 4. Labor laws and
legislation—Canada. 5. Comparative law. I. Roberts, Karen. II.
Clarke, Ronald O. (Ronald Oliver) III. Title.
  HD8072.5.B57 2002
  331.12'042'0973—dc21

                              2002013604

Cover design by J.R. Underhill.
Index prepared by Nancy Humphreys.
Printed in the United States of America.
Printed on recycled paper.

Dedication

This book is dedicated to our late colleague and coauthor, R. Oliver Clarke, 1923–2001. Upon his death in August, 2001, Professor Greg Bamber of Griffith University in Australia circulated the following biography of Oliver:

> Oliver Clarke was a Visiting Professor at Michigan State University's School of Labor and Industrial Relations. He also had visiting assignments at the universities of: British Columbia, Wisconsin-Madison, Western Australia, New South Wales, South Australia, Leuven, Curtin University of Technology, Perth, and also the American Graduate School of International Management, Arizona. After working in industry, where he trained in engineering, he became Secretary of the EEF, a major British employers' association. Then, after a period as Research Fellow at the London School of Economics and as a management consultant, he served for eighteen years in the Organization for Economic Cooperation and Development in Paris, where he coordinated its work on industrial relations. He published widely on various aspects of IR.

Few people in the field were as expert as Oliver in matters involving international industrial relations, as the many students who took his courses will attest. Indeed, his knowledge was truly encyclopedic, as was evidenced by his annual article on labor matters for the Encyclopedia Britannica. Thus, Oliver touched academics, students, and the general public.

On a sabbatical in London in the winter of 2001, I had the pleasure of spending many Thursday mornings with Oliver when illness confined him to his house in London's Golders Green. We discussed industrial relations in Britain, the United States, and the European Union. Oliver pushed my thinking on U.S. industrial relations and labor matters, always encouraging me to remember that the U.S. system of employment is only one of many in the world. Perhaps we in the United States, he always pointed out, could learn something from others. Oliver's colleagues and his students are wiser and more insightful for having known and been taught by him. He is missed.

R.N.B.

Contents

Figure

Tables

Acknowledgments

This work is an attempt to measure and quantify a range of labor standards in the United States and Canada. It is the first step in answering a series of questions that has long interested academics, practitioners, and policymakers: Do labor standards matter, and if so, for what? Do high labor standards adversely affect overall economic growth and employment because they make it difficult for firms in high standards jurisdictions to compete? And, do high labor standards result in improved worker welfare? In order to reach an answer to these questions, it is necessary to first create a measure of labor standards so that the differences in these standards can be measured across jurisdictions. This work makes a first attempt to create such a measurement.

Because any such system of measures is subject to debate, challenge, and discussion, not only have we provided our measures of labor standards, but the W.E. Upjohn Institute has also made the data accessible on a website (<www.upjohninstitute.org/BlockRoberts>). This will permit others not only to use the measures, but also to adjust or change them as they see fit. It is our hope that the data will be used, and that other researchers will improve and refine our measures.

This work was supported by the International Center for Canadian-American Trade (ICCAT); the city of Port Huron, Michigan (through a grant from the United States Department of State); the Canadian Embassy in the United States; and the W.E. Upjohn Institute for Employment Research. This book represents the views of the authors and does not necessarily represent the views of ICCAT, the United States Department of State, the Canadian Government, or the W.E. Upjohn Institute for Employment Research. The authors wish to thank Jennifer Evans, Kellie Henehan, Drew Hoffman, Patrick Hughes, Michael Leland, Steven Leonoff, Natasha Kehimkar, Jeonghyn Lee, Jennifer Lombardo, Jonathan McDermott, Suzanne Monahan, Christine Normoyle, Cynthia Ozeki, Jane Spooner, Allen Venable, Jennifer Werner, and Stephen Whitaker for their research assistance. We also thank Randy Smadella from Statistics Canada for providing employment data. Veronique Marleau provided guidance and insight into Canadian labor standards. Kevin Hollenbeck, Mary Pavlock, Frances Emery, Leslie Lance, and Richard Wyrwa—all from the W.E. Upjohn Institute for Employment Research—were essential to guiding the project through publication, in addition to undertaking a massive editing job and developing the website. We thank them. Any errors are, of course, our own.

1
Introduction

Whereas the League of Nations has for its object the establishment of universal peace, and such a peace can be established only
if it is based upon social justice;

And whereas conditions of labour exist involving such injus-
tice, hardship, and privation to large numbers of people as to produce unrest so great that the peace and harmony of the world are
imperilled; and an improvement of those conditions is urgently
required: as, for example, by the regulation of the hours of work,
including the establishment of a maximum working day and
week, the regulation of the labour supply, the prevention of unemployment, the provision of an adequate living wage, the protection
of the worker against sickness, disease and injury arising out of
his employment, the protection of children, young persons and
women, provision for old age and injury, protection of the interests of workers when employed in countries other than their own,
recognition of the principle of freedom of association, the organi-
sation of vocational and technical education and other measures;

Whereas also the failure of any nation to adopt humane conditions of labour is an obstacle in the way of other nations which
desire to improve the conditions in their own countries; . . .

Treaty of Versailles, 1919

The above quotation, from the provision of the Treaty of Versailles
establishing the International Labor Office in 1919, illustrates that the
issue of international labor standards has long been on the world stage.
During the last two decades, however, rising levels of international
trade and a proliferation of large-scale trade agreements have increased
the level of attention on cross-country differences in labor standards
and on issues associated with setting and enforcing international labor
standards. Much of the discussion is on the interrelationship between
international trade and labor standards. Despite considerable public
attention, relatively little empirical research has studied this relationship. One reason for this empirical void is the difficulty associated
with developing reliable measures of labor standards.

This volume has two purposes. The primary purpose is to begin to fill the gap in the research by developing a measure of labor standards that can be applied across countries. A second purpose is to apply that measure to the United States and Canada to test a popular hypothesis that Canada has higher labor standards than those in the United States.[1]

OVERVIEW OF THE RECENT DISCUSSION OF LABOR STANDARDS AND INTERNATIONAL TRADE

As international trade continues to rise, so does the awareness of labor standards at global, regional, and national levels. The debate over the legitimacy of international labor standards and of linking standards to trade agreements has been long and contentious. This debate represents a deeper concern than simply identifying the "winners and losers" in free trade. Rather, it focuses on the role of government policy in protecting citizen welfare. Government policy on employment issues, like most government domestic policy, has traditionally been determined by the domestic values as expressed in the political process. In an insular world with no outside contacts, societies could adopt economic and employment relations policies solely in accordance with their national interests and value systems, with little concern about the consequences of interaction with societies having different economic structures, employment relations, or value systems. In a world of free trade, however, the insularity assumption does not hold. As competition increases, firms are more likely to be under pressure to view human resources as a factor of production affecting their ability to compete in the product market. In their attempts to become more competitive, firms may be tempted to use free trade to escape costly regulatory obligations by moving production to a location with less burdensome and, therefore, less costly labor standards. Labor conditions in different countries are thereby placed into competition. Labor and employment policy, once exclusively a domestic issue, is now affected by outside forces.

Differences in labor standards and labor employment policy among competitors received little attention when the primary competitors were firms in developed countries—the United States, Canada,

Western Europe, and Japan—because all were perceived to be high-wage countries, with high labor standards. When less developed countries began to compete, however, with their lower labor standards and lower wage rates, labor standards in competing countries began to be seen as sources of competitive disadvantage for the developed countries.

Despite the intense public debate and interest that labor standards issues have aroused over the last decade, there has been almost no research on the relationship between trade and labor standards. A primary reason for this empirical gap is the absence of measures of labor standards that can be applied internationally.

The first objective of this book is to begin to close this empirical gap by presenting a new method for comparing labor standards across political jurisdictions; the second is to apply that method to the United States and Canada. In the absence of reliable comparative measures, there is no way of evaluating differences in labor standards among countries. Therefore, there is no way of knowing how such differences affect trade flows or other economic outcomes, such as income distribution and employment levels.

THE SOCIAL CONTEXTS: WHY CANADA AND THE UNITED STATES MAY DIVERGE

When the issue of a free trade arrangement with the United States and Canada was initially raised, one commonly articulated concern was that Canadian labor standards would be forced downward as Canadian and U.S. producers began to compete openly (Langille 1991). Several years before the Free Trade Agreement was signed, the Canadian Minister for International Trade, Gerald Regan, articulated the basis for proceeding with the negotiations by saying, "I am convinced above all that we cannot stand still and must explore new alternatives to preserve and expand market access . . . The status quo is simply not a viable option for Canada's future."[2] One basis for the opposition to a free trade agreement was the belief that Canada had higher labor standards than the United States, and that the low labor standards of new U.S. firms would give those firms a competitive advantage vis-à-vis their Canadian counterparts. It was feared that free trade would result in job losses or a deterioration of standards in Canada.

The second objective of this volume is to compare labor standards in the United States and Canada and to examine the question of whether labor standards are higher in Canada than in the United States. Canada and the United States form a particularly interesting comparison because the two countries are quite similar in both economic and demographic structure, yet differ in employment outcomes in several important ways.

The United States and Canada are neighbors and one another's largest trading partners. Among their similarities, both are developed Western countries that trace their origins to British rule in the 18th century. Neither nation suffered economic infrastructure damage or civilian casualties during World War II. Thus, the industrial structures and labor forces of the two countries are similar.

In terms of industrial structure, the plant, and equipment in the two countries have followed comparable development cycles since World War II. In fact, many firms operate on both sides of the border (Lipset 1989; Rugman 1991). The employment distribution across industries differs in several ways, however. While both economies employ approximately 15 percent of the workforce in manufacturing and 17 to 18 percent in trade, the service sector in Canada constitutes 38 percent of employment, compared with about 24 percent in the United States. Another difference is that Canadian employment is somewhat more concentrated in primary industries, including logging and forestry, fishing and trapping, and mining. Primary industries employ 2.1 percent of the Canadian workforce, compared with 0.5 percent in the United States (CANSIM 1998; U.S. Department of Commerce 1998e).

In general, the compositions of both the populations and the labor forces of the two countries are fairly similar. First, the populations have similar age distributions. In Canada, 33.2 percent of the population are under 25 and 12.3 percent are age 65 or older (CANSIM 1998). In the United States, 35.5 percent of the population is under 25, and 12.8 percent are 65 or over (U.S. Department of Commerce 1998c). Labor force participation is slightly higher in the United States: 79.3 percent compared with 75.9 percent in Canada, in 1996 (CANSIM 1998). Although these rates are nearly identical for prime-aged males and females (ages 25 to 54) in the two countries (about 91 percent for males and 76 percent for females), labor force attachment for U.S. workers is distinctly higher for those over 55. In Canada, the labor force participation rates of males ages of 55 to 64 and those 65 or over are 59.3 percent and 10.3 percent, respectively. The comparable rates in the United States are 67.0 percent and 16.6 percent. There are similar patterns for females: the rates for Canadian women 55 to 64 and 65 or over are 39.6 percent and 3.5 percent, respectively, compared with 49.6 percent and 8.6 percent in the United States.[3]

Both countries are experiencing an ethnic diversification of their populations, as both have been the destinations of European and more recently Asian immigrants (Borjas 1993). Canada's share of immigrants from Asia is, however, effectively twice that of the United States: over 1995–1996, 65.9 percent of all Canadian immigrants were from Asia, compared with 37.2 percent for the United States in 1995 (CANSIM 1998; U.S. Department of Commerce 1998b). In contrast, a much larger share of U.S. immigrants comes from Mexico and Central America: 30.3 percent of U.S. immigrants compared with 1.5 percent of Canadian immigrants.

The education levels of the two countries' populations are roughly comparable, although tight comparisons are difficult because of differences in the degree structure and because government data are reported for different age categories. In Canada, 17 percent of those aged 20 or over have a university degree, compared with 15.8 percent of those aged 25 and over in the United States, suggesting that the Canadian labor force is better educated. However, only 18 percent of Canadians aged 15 and over have just high school diplomas, compared with 33.6 percent of the U.S. population aged 25 years or older, suggesting that the U.S. labor force may be better educated (Statistics Canada 1998; U.S. Department of Commerce 1998d).

Despite these broad similarities, researchers have noted differences in several labor market outcomes. One difference is in unemployment. Until the recession of the early 1980s, the two countries experienced almost identical unemployment rates (Card and Freeman 1993; Riddell and Sharpe 1998).[4] Since then, Canada has experienced chronically higher unemployment rates relative to the United States. On average, over the 1983–1996 period, the unemployment rate in the United States was 6.5 percent, compared with 9.8 percent in Canada (Nickell 1997). This difference has increased during the 1990s, with short-term unemployment falling in the United States from 6.4 percent between 1983 and 1988 to 5.6 percent between 1989 and 1994, while the comparable Canadian rate remained effectively constant—9 percent in the early period, 8.9 percent in the later period (Nickell 1997). Subgroup unemployment rates in 1996 indicate that unemployment for those just entering the labor market, ages 15 to 24, and those on the verge of leaving, age 65 or over, is nearly identical in the two countries. However, Canada's unemployment rate for prime age workers, 25 to 54, is approximately twice that in the United States.

Economists speculate about reasons for this difference in unemployment rates. One ready explanation is that wages are more flexible in the United States than in most developed countries, implying that the U.S. labor market equilibrates through adjustments in wages rather than employment levels. Time series data do not support this explanation, however; they suggest, in fact, that wages are less flexible in both the U.S. and Canadian labor markets than in other developed economies, and that, comparing the two countries, U.S. wages are slightly less flexible than those in Canada (Nickell 1997). In addition, research comparing Canada, the United States, and France suggests that wage rigidity does not explain employment growth differences, implying that it also will not explain unemployment differences (Card, Kramarz, and Lemieux 1996).

There seems to be some agreement that the reasons for the unemployment rate gap in the 1980s are different from those for the 1990s (Keil and Pantuosco 1998; Riddell and Sharpe 1998). For example, one explanation that has been explored is that the gap is the result of different rates of economic growth, attributable to differing monetary policies in the two countries. Evidence shows that the two countries had comparable rates of growth through the 1980s, but that over the period from 1989 through 1996, the annual growth rate in gross domestic product (GDP) in the United States was 1.9 percent compared with 1.2 percent in Canada. This suggests that, while a macroeconomic explanation is plausible for the 1990s, it is probably not so for the initial gap in the 1980s.

Card and Freeman (1993) empirically decomposed the unemployment rate difference during the 1980s and conclude that it can be attributed to structural features in the two labor markets. They note that the labor force participation for females increased faster in Canada than in the United States in the early 1980s, and that this increase took the form of longer unemployment durations. They link this behavior change to two aspects of unemployment insurance in Canada: the availability of maternity leave benefits associated with unemployment or employment insurance and the substantially higher take-up rates—approximately 60 percent in Canada compared with 25 percent in the United States (Card and Freeman 1993). Increases in female participation rates in Canada have also been interpreted as having caused increasing unemployment rates in Canada by allowing other household members to extend their job searches (Keil and Pantuosco 1998). This is consistent with other findings showing that the 1981–1993 gap can be explained in part by longer unemployment durations on the part of Canadian males (Tille 1998).

A second difference is in the union density rates in the two countries. Compiling data from the U.S. Current Population Survey and the Canadian Labour Market Activity Survey, Dinardo and Lemieux (1997) found overall union density rates of 21.4 percent and 40.2 percent in 1988 for the United States and Canada, respectively. In the labor force aged 25 and over, there is a consistent difference in the rates of 20 percentage points between the two countries for all age groups, indicating that this difference is not a cohort effect. Although within all educational categories Canadians are more likely than Americans to be union members, the largest difference is for the most educated, those with 16 years of school or more: in 1988, 13.9 percent of such U.S. workers were union members, compared with 35.7 percent of similarly educated Canadians. While there are some differences in industry mix, they do not explain the differences in union density rates. Rather, Canadian workers in every industry are more likely to be union members than are their counterparts in the United States. Current data suggest that the differences in union density rates persist.

A third labor market outcome in which the United States and Canada have diverged is that of income inequality. The increasing inequality of income in the United States has been well documented (Gottschalk and Moffitt 1994; Johnson 1998; Topel 1997), but whereas the Canadian evidence suggests that income inequality increased during the late 1960s and again in the early 1980s, the evidence of rising inequality is ambiguous in Canada since the early 1980s (Blackburn and Bloom 1993). Beach and Slotsve (1996) argued that, contrary to popular opinion, there is no evidence of income polarization in Canada. They maintained that increases in income inequality in Canada can be accounted for almost entirely by cyclical factors, and that there is a tight correlation between the unemployment rate and income inequality. Further, they found that income inequality for women, while higher than for men, actually declined over the 1971–1992 period.

When the focus shifts to earnings, however, polarization is more evident. Again, there is evidence of gender differences: earnings inequality did increase for males but decreased for females. Beach and Slotsve find different underlying patterns for men and women. There appears to be a long-term trend toward decreased inequality for women; however, male inequality seems to be more a function of economic growth and unemployment rates. These differences combined with Canadian income transfer policies have meant that there have been no real long-term changes in family income inequality, unlike the situation in the United States.

These observations are supported by another study, which finds that increased hours of work by families mitigated against factors that increased inequality in Canada (Morissette, Myles, and Picot 1995). That study did find evidence of increased income inequality in Canada but attributes it to differences in the hours worked, with more people working part time, and those working full time working more than 40 hours. This contrasts with the explanation commonly given for inequality in the United States—that is, that widening gaps in the number of years of education and in the quality of education lead to differences in earnings.

Unlike Beach and Slotsve, however, Morissette et al. argued that there are underlying trends in the rise of income inequality that cannot be entirely explained by the business cycle. Their interpretation of the shift in hours of work distribution is that firms are adopting a core-contingent workforce strategy, increasing the number of hours worked by core workers and decreasing the number worked by contingent workers.

In a comparative study of how technological change has affected the wage distribution in the United States and Canada, Murphy et al. (1998) also attributed the differences between the two countries to income transfer policies. Their study differs from most in that they examine this relationship in two ways. First, they maintain that differences in labor supply at relative wage rates can affect inequality and that these are omitted from most studies. Second, they note that usually a technological explanation of wage inequality explains abrupt shifts in the wage distribution and not smooth trends. They argued that the differences in shifts in the income distribution in the two countries can be explained by an "education-race" model, and that differences in social policy between Canada and the United States explain the outcome differences.

The education-race model argues that there are two simultaneous trends, one driven by rates of technological change and the other by changes in the education distribution of the workforce. During the period under study, 1963–1994, Murphy et al. assumed a constant rate of technological change (that is, change due to the introduction of the digital computer) and then examined how the relative supply of high school versus college educated workers has affected the income distribution. They provided evidence that, cumulatively, technological change has increased the demand for more educated workers relative to their supply and has thus increased the earnings inequality. However, the income transfer policies in Canada have mitigated that effect such that income inequality there has not increased as it has in the United States.

One explanation for some of these differences in the various economic outcomes may lie in the fact that the United States and Canada differ in their views of the relationship between the individual and the government and of the role of the state in regulating economic matters. The United States is generally considered antistatist and individualistic (Lipset 1989; Blank 1994; Block 1992). Its entire constitutional and governmental structure is built around limiting the power and role of government. Canada is more statist than the United States, and has traditionally been more willing to accept some governmental control over the lives of its citizens in order to obtain security and order (White 1988; Lipset 1989). Therefore, as a society, Canadians are likely to be more willing than citizens of the United States to use the government as an instrument of wealth redistribution.

This difference in values between the United States and Canada toward the role of the state was manifested most clearly in the debate around the 1988 Canada-U.S. Free Trade Agreement.[5] The FTA generated far more public debate in Canada than in the United States (Mahant 1993). Canadian opponents of the FTA made their arguments in terms of sovereignty, holding that Canada's commitment to a high level of social welfare for all its citizens would be compromised if free trade resulted in pressure to harmonize its policies downward with U.S. policies (Lyon 1987; Doern and Tomlin 1991; Martin 1991; Mahant 1993; Smith 1988).

A key theme in that debate was the perceived Canadian commitment to social welfare in the form of high labor standards.[6] The concern on the part of Canadian FTA opponents seemed to be that, to assure competitiveness in the product market, Canadian firms could use the pressure of free trade as a basis for a political attempt to unburden themselves of labor standards obligations, could reduce compensation to offset the costs of the higher Canadian labor standards, or could move production to a location that was believed to have less burdensome and therefore, less costly labor standards. In all cases, the welfare of workers and citizens would be reduced through a reduction in standards, in compensation, or in employment.

That view is based on the assumption that Canada's labor standards are superior to those of the United States, an assumption that is one component of a more general attitude that Canada is more generous than the United States in all forms of social assistance, in terms of both eligibility and level of benefits (Blank and Hanratty 1993). Empirical comparisons of social assistance programs in the two countries, however, present a mixed picture. Part of this arises from the differing degrees to which these programs are federally controlled in the two countries, with Canadian policies generally emanating from the provinces, and U.S. policies reflecting more of a federal-state mix (Boychuk 1997). As the United States experienced growth during the 1960s and 1970s in federal antipoverty programs, Canadian federal policy took a cost-sharing form of matching provincial benefits that allowed for considerable interprovincial variation (Blank and Hanratty 1993).

More recently, both countries have experienced a backlash against spending on social assistance. In the United States, this has taken the form of some federal retrenchment, leading to more interstate variation. Empirical comparisons of social assistance in the two countries suggest that, on average, both coverage and benefit levels are more generous in Canada than in the United States, but that there is sufficient variation that, depending on the program feature, the least (most) generous Canadian province is less generous than the least (most) generous U.S. state (Blank and Hanratty 1993; Boychuk 1997).

A second objective of this monograph is to investigate whether the conventional wisdom, that Canadian labor standards are higher than in the United States and that the difference is substantive, is correct. The chief justification for asking such questions is that a finding of substantive and significant differences would allow the investigation of the economic effect of the level of labor standards on various economic outcomes. It is often held that higher labor standards would put domestic firms at a disadvantage relative to their foreign counterparts, other things (such as exchange rates) being equal. It is also plausible that higher governmentally mandated labor standards might induce firms to invest in their workforces (that is, engage in an efficiency wage strategy) and thus raise the productivity of labor relative to foreign competitors. The extent to which Canadian labor standards are actually higher than U.S. standards has never been demonstrated. Our empirical examination of this issue will allow us to test the validity of the assumption—often political—that labor standards are a cost, putting domestic producers at a competitive disadvantage.

ORGANIZATION

This publication is associated with a website that makes available the data used to measure the labor standards in the two countries. This availability will permit researchers throughout the world to use the data to replicate our results, to change the assumptions underlying our results, or to apply specific standards that may interest them and analyze their impact on trade and trade-related phenomena. This website will also permit researchers to easily use or adapt this method to compare labor standards across jurisdictions other than the United States and Canada.

Turning to the organization of this volume, Chapter 2 reviews the literature on the relationship between labor standards and trade, both generally and with specific attention to the United States and Canada. Chapter 3 provides definitions of the labor standards discussed. Chapter 4 discusses the data and methodology used to compare the labor standards in the two countries. Chapter 5 presents the results of the comparison of labor standards in the two countries, through text and tables. Chapter 6 summarizes the results and presents conclusions.

Notes

1. Not all work finds that U.S. labor costs are lower than those in Canada. One study (Roberts and Smith 1992) found that U.S. and Canadian labor costs were quite comparable. Expressed in U.S. dollars, in 1993 the average hourly compensation for production workers in manufacturing stood at $16.79 in the United States and $16.36 in Canada, further suggesting comparability between the two countries (U.S. Department of Labor 1994a). To the extent that labor standards are reflected in hourly compensation, this research should cause one to question the proposition that Canadian firms are at a disadvantage relative to their counterparts in the United States.
2. Regan 1984, p. 16.
3. It could be argued that higher social welfare benefits in Canada explain some of the differences in labor force participation. However, research on the labor force participation decision in Canada shows that it depends more on personal characteristics than on the level of welfare benefits (Christofides, Stengos, and Swidinsky 1997).
4. Although the gap between Canadian and U.S. unemployment rates has triggered considerable interest among economists, there is some evidence that the relationship between the two rates, including the almost identical patterns up until the early 1980s, is a statistical artifact, and that looking for structural shifts or exogenous shocks to explain the gap is misguided (Lang and Zagorsky 1998).
5. The discussion in this paper focuses on the debate around the 1988 FTA. Although many of the same issues were raised in the debate around the 1993 North American Free Trade Agreement (NAFTA) involving Canada, Mexico, and the United States, the fact that NAFTA involved a third, less-developed country made it more difficult to focus on that debate in discussing Canadian-U.S. differences.
6. There has been some work on specific issues that might be considered labor standards. For comparative studies in collective bargaining, see Weiler (1983), Adams (1993), and Block (1994 and 1996). For comparative studies in workers' compensation, see Burton (1989), Roberts and Madden (1992), and Hyatt and Kralj (1992). For a comparative study in unjust discharge, see Jain (1992). For an overview of social contracts, see Card and Freeman (1994).

2
Labor Standards and Trade

Background and Literature Review

Two distinct, but related, bodies of literature discuss the interrelationship between trade and labor standards. The economics literature treats labor standards as a form of factor price and examines, in that light, how labor standards affect trade and vice versa. The institutional literature debates, first, whether labor standards should be explicitly linked to trade agreements and, second, the propriety of setting universal standards. This chapter provides an overview of these two discussions.

The following section of this chapter reviews the economics perspective on labor standards, discussing three branches of the literature: first, the studies on how factor prices affect trade, then those on how trade affects factor outcomes, and finally, the few studies on the relationship between labor standards and trade. The next section, a discussion of the institutional perspective, expands the concept of labor standards to examine the literature on universal labor standards, both the studies that support explicit linkages between trade arrangements and those that oppose such linkages. The chapter concludes with an overview of two preeminent institutions that establish and attempt to enforce international labor standards: the International Labour Organization (ILO) and the European Union (EU). The EU analysis centers on the experience of Germany, the United Kingdom, and Sweden.

THE ECONOMIC PERSPECTIVE

The relationship between trade and factor prices is complicated and not especially well understood. One source of complexity is that causality can be argued either way: trade flows can depend on factor prices (which affect product prices); but also factor prices can shift when reducing trade restrictions increases competition. Considerable research has been done on the determinants of trade. Similarly, the effect of trade on factor prices, particularly wages, has been investigated. However, an important gap remains in this research: the relationship between trade and labor standards, as a form of factor price, has not been thoroughly investigated.

The Effect of Factor Price on Trade

The simplest understanding of trade is based on the theory of comparative advantage, in which parties trade those goods for which they have the relative production cost advantage (Karier 1991; Krugman 1994). In the comparative advantage model, countries differ in productivity and factor price but not in factor endowments. If trade barriers are dropped, trade occurs because each country can specialize according to its relative productivity. The resulting more efficient use of resources lowers prices for traded goods, and producers from both countries face the improved demand schedule resulting from aggregating across the trading units as well as the reduced product price resulting from more efficient production.

The welfare implications of the comparative advantage model are unambiguous: both trading parties enter the exchange voluntarily and do so only because each is better off than it would be in the absence of trade (Marshall 1994). The comparative advantage model views any sort of tariff or nontariff barriers to free trade as reducing the efficiency of market allocation of resources, and thus, as suboptimal.[1] According to this view, although protectionist tactics may provide short-term benefits to selective groups, both trading partners are better off under conditions of unrestricted trade (Gaston and Trefler 1994). Free trade permits welfare to be maximized in both the importing and the exporting country, because each country will be better off than otherwise (Srinivasan 1995; Brown, Deardorff, and Stern 1997; Golub 1997).

In a solely domestic context (referred to as an autarky), government-mandated labor standards can be seen from the employer perspective as a universally imposed cost of production, and from the employee perspective as a set of protections of income or quality of work life. Once trade is introduced and the economy becomes more competitive, the cost aspect of labor standards loses its universality.

Producers located in jurisdictions where labor standards are high often perceive themselves as facing higher production costs than those faced by their low-labor-standard competitors. In fact, in the debate over linking labor standards to trade agreements such as the General Agreement on Tariffs and Trade (GATT), developing countries often accuse developed countries of advocating labor standards obligations in order to diminish the production advantage that the developing country has because of its lower labor costs (Swinnerton and Schoepfle 1994).

From this perspective, statutory protection of the workforce can be viewed by producers as a nontariff trade barrier. Advocates of the comparative advantage framework may acknowledge that certain dislocations will occur in the short run, with less-efficient producers and their employees suffering as a result of competition from more efficient producers. Proponents of this view further argue that unimpeded growth could result in better working conditions and higher wages than if labor standards were legislated (Hufbauer and Schot 1992).

Proponents of labor standards raise several counterarguments, all designed to show that the imposition of labor standards does not necessarily harm the competitive position of international traders. One is that cost minimization is not necessarily the most efficient production strategy, at least with regard to labor costs. This argument is based on the efficiency wage theory (Carmichael 1989). Efficiency wage theory argues that employees and employers strike a wage-effort bargain, in which employees will put forth greater effort in exchange for long-term higher wages. Efficiency wage theory has important implications for many aspects of the employment relationship, but the one relevant to trade is that this theory provides an economic justification for employers paying what appears to be above-market wages while remaining competitive in the product market. According to this model, firms are seen as making a strategic choice as to how to operate. The choice to pay above-market wages and invest in workers is an attribute of a "high-performance" workplace (Appelbaum and Batt 1994; Marshall 1994). Thus, one economic justification for labor standards is that they are part of a high-compensation strategy that induces high levels of work effort or low levels of employee monitoring, and so does not harm the competitiveness of producers in the product market (Sharma and Giles 1994; Groshen and Krueger 1990).

A second justification for labor standards comes out of the consumer theory (Freeman 1994). According to that view, labor standards can be seen as a consumer good and a normal good in that demand increases with wealth. In the autarky framework, the level of labor standards could easily be seen as an indication of that society's willingness to pay for a workplace that is safer, more just, more secure, or having some other welfare-enhancing quality. There are three likely payers for these standards: employees who pay in the form of lower wages,[2] consumers who pay in the form of higher product prices, and taxpayers who pay in the form of higher taxes. In the world of imperfect competition, it is also possible that firms (or their shareholders) would pay in the form of lower monopoly profits (Karier 1992). With the introduction of trade, labor standards become components of the product price; thus, consumers, employees, and taxpayers express their willingness to pay for the higher labor standards by their acceptance of the higher-priced goods, the lower wages, or the higher taxes.[3]

Empirical analyses of the effects of various factors thought to affect the cost of labor on trade flows or other measures of economic growth give a mixed picture. Karier (1991, 1992, 1995) examined the effect of union density on the U.S. trade deficit and found no union effect. Cooke (1997) examined the effects of various measures of the industrial relations climate on direct foreign investment in countries within the Organization for Economic Co-operation and Development (OECD) and found that investment was negatively affected by union density rates, centralized collective bargaining structures, and government regulations on layoff procedures, but positively affected by human capital levels of the workforce and mechanisms for joint labor-management cooperation. Several studies have examined the effects of union density rates on capital investment and found a negative (usually nonlinear) relationship (Hirsch 1992; Odgers and Betts 1997). Sharma and Giles (1994) examined whether income policies, collectively bargained wage rates, and statutory reduction in working time affected a country's export levels and its share of the world's export markets. Using data from 10 countries over a 20-year period, they found limited support for a negative effect of bargained wage rates on trade, no effect for working time regulation, and negative and significant effects of income policies on trade.

The Effect of Trade on Factors of Production

The concern about the effects of free trade on factors of production (in the labor context—employment, wages, and labor standards) is that the competition in the product market will force producers to engage in a cost-minimization strategy that will result in lower wages, less employment, or both. The specific concerns are that global competition will result in higher unemployment and falling relative wages for lower-skilled workers, and thus rising wage inequality, deterioration of labor standards, and a decline in national autonomy in setting standards that are consistent with each country's values (Adams 1997; Lee 1997).

In a version of the comparative advantage model, trade occurs as a result of different factor endowments that result in different factor prices. These differences in factor prices form the basis for a comparative advantage. In this model, free trade in goods will equalize factor prices across countries as international flows of factors or technology lead to the convergence of endowments and thus of factor price (Slaughter 1997). In the case of labor standards, while trade may not lead directly to convergence of labor standards, this model predicts political pressures in that direction (Compa 1993).

Few empirical studies directly examine the relationship between trade liberalization and labor standards. Most of the empirical work examines the effect of trade on other aspects of work, such as wages, employment, or income distribution. Again, empirical studies provide mixed results. For example, some research supports the assertion that growing earnings inequality within developed countries can be partly attributed to increased international trade (Borjas and Ramey 1994; Richardson 1995). Wood (1995) examined income distribution in developed countries and found that relative wages for unskilled workers in those countries had deteriorated as a result of trade with developing countries. Additional evidence suggests that both import and export activity increase earnings inequality, but that import activity has the greater effect (Borjas and Ramey 1994).

In contrast to those studies, Edwards (1997) examined changes in income distribution for developing countries as a proxy for this outcome and found no increase in income inequality as a result of trade liberalization. Ben-David (1993) found evidence for a positive relationship between trade liberalization and income convergence, but

Slaughter (1997) noted that, although theory predicts that trade liberalization should lead to the convergence of income across trading partners, income convergence can be predicted as easily by a convergence in worker's access to capital stock as by trade liberalization.

In an examination of Canadian income distribution, Richardson (1997) compared wage distributions in the United States and Canada from 1981 through 1992. His comparison showed that male wage inequality grew at a faster rate in the United States for the 1981–1989 period. But, inequality increased much more in Canada between 1989 and 1992. Richardson does not discuss this in terms of the implementation of the Free Trade Agreement (FTA); however, the timing of the change in relative inequality does coincide with the implementation of the agreement.

Several studies on the effects of trade liberalization on unemployment show results that parallel those studies cited above that find an increasing inequality of income distribution. Three studies of the displacement effects of trade suggest that employees who lose their jobs in trade-sensitive industries experience unemployment spells of longer duration than those losing jobs from trade-insensitive industries (Addison, Fox, and Ruhm 1995; Bednarzik 1993; Kruse 1988). This is consistent with the results of another study that showed that trade-related employment gains in the service sector were most likely to be found in skill-intensive services (Armah 1994). Lee (1997) concluded, however, in his discussion of the labor issues associated with economic integration, that the balance of the empirical evidence cannot support the hypothesis that trade is a primary explanation for rising unemployment.

Empirical Research on Trade and Labor Standards

Some empirical work has been done on the relationship between labor standards and trade. Rodrick (1994) used a measure of a country's labor standards that was composed of the following indicators: the number of total ILO conventions and the number of basic rights ILO conventions ratified, indicators of political and civil rights, indicators of the extent of the annual enforcement of child labor legislation, the number of statutory hours of work in manufacturing or construction, the number of days of annual leave in manufacturing, and the percentage of the labor force that was unionized.

Rodrick found that the convention ratification measures and the rights measure were positively and significantly related to labor costs, whereas the child labor measure generated a negative and significant coefficient. Gross national product (GNP) per worker was used as a control measure of productivity. With the exception of the number of hours of work, however, Rodrick did not find that the labor standards were positively related to a comparative advantage in labor-intensive goods as measured by the ratio of textile and clothing exports to all non-fuel exports.

Aggarwal (1995a) examined export and investment data for countries and sectors considered to have varying levels of labor standards. She found that for Singapore, Mexico, South Korea, and Malaysia—countries she considered "developing"—more than half the export share was accounted for by machines and transport equipment, industries that were considered to have higher labor standards than textiles, garments, and toys. The latter industries, however, were within the top five export sectors for those countries. Examining U.S. direct foreign investment in nine developing countries, she found no indication that such investment went disproportionately to labor-intensive industries. She also concluded that developing countries with low labor standards have a small aggregate impact on U.S. imports. In 1994, ten developing countries accounted for 26.5 percent of U.S. total imports, whereas Canada, Germany, France, the United Kingdom, and Japan accounted for 51.1 percent of imports. She did point out, however, that at the current growth rates the import share from developing countries would have risen to approximately 41.5 percent by the year 2000. She also found no evidence of employment or wage declines in U.S. sectors producing goods commonly associated with low labor standards in response to the imports from developing countries.

The OECD (1996) examined the relationship between freedom of association and trade. Countries were divided into four groups on the basis of each country's ratification of ILO conventions, with group 1 manifesting the broadest rights of freedom of association, and group 4 the narrowest. Using a one-way visual analysis, the study found no indication that freedom of association was related to the change in the country's share of world exports between 1980 and 1990, but some indication that countries that had greater restrictions on freedom of association experienced an increase in the country's share of world manufacturing imports. Improvement in labor standards seemed to have no effect on export performance. Although there was evidence that countries with narrow rights of freedom of association had lower export prices for textiles, the group 1 countries had the highest market share, suggesting the possibility of product differentiation. There was no evidence that high labor standards affected foreign direct investment (FDI); in 1993, 73 percent of FDI went to the high-standards OECD countries.

There are limitations to these three studies. The OECD study focused only on one indicator of labor standards: freedom of association. Although Rodrick's work used multiple indicators, these were measured only in the broadest way, by ratification of ILO conventions. Aggarwal's work relied principally on judgments of countries considered to have high or low labor standards.

THE INSTITUTIONAL PERSPECTIVE

In the political arena, the coupling of labor standards with free trade issues has been the subject of long-standing discussion over the past 100 years (Charnovitz 1987; French 1994). Before the 1980s, much of the discussion was raised in the context of competition among countries at roughly similar levels of economic development (Servais 1989). The issue took on renewed urgency in the 1980s, however, with the increased involvement in worldwide trade of less-developed, third world countries (Servais 1989). Since the Uruguay Round in 1986, where the coupling was formally raised in a trade context (Charnovitz 1987; OECD 1996), a theoretical and conceptual literature has emerged on linking labor standards to free trade agreements.

The theoretical and conceptual literature consists of two competing viewpoints. One, associated primarily although not totally with the ILO, is generally sympathetic to a legal linkage of trade and labor standards. The second, associated primarily with advocates for less-developed countries, takes the position that it is inappropriate to link the trade privileges of a country with the labor standards of that country.

Linking Trade and Labor Standards

Although concern about the relationship between labor standards and international trade has a long history, was referenced in the GATT, and has been an integral aspect of the European Union (Hansson 1983), that concern increased in the 1970s, when a long recession in the industrialized market economies coincided with increased worldwide productive capacity in such labor-intensive industries as apparel, textiles, shoes, and electronics (Edgren 1979).

Those sympathetic to the position that there should be a social clause in trade agreements or a procedure in the worldwide trading system that would link trade privileges to internal labor standards base their position on human rights and social values. If a country wishes to reap the benefits of participating in the world trading system, then that country should be obliged to guarantee its workers at least a minimal acceptable level of labor standards (Maier 1994; ICFTU 1996; Caire 1994; Emmerij 1994).

These arguments have sparked discussion of the propriety of incorporating a social clause or labor standards requirements in the international trading system. It has been pointed out that a series of declarations sanctioned by the United Nations are consistent with the principle that there should be a balance among markets, open information, and government action; therefore, government action may be essential to protecting worker rights in social development, thus creating a role for labor standards enforcement in the trading system (de Waart 1996). It is argued that requiring some minimal level of labor standards would promote fair competition; firms would not be able to use the lower labor standards and living conditions in some countries to cause lower wages or less employment in the importing country or in the country from which employment is shifted. This, in turn, would prevent any downward harmonizing of labor standards from causing a "race to the bottom" and "social dumping" (Charnovitz 1987; van Liemt 1989; Langille 1994; Gunderson 1998).

It is also argued that a social clause diffuses the benefits from trade, increasing the possibility that workers worldwide will benefit from trade, rather than some workers benefiting, and other workers being victimized (van Liemt 1989; Golub 1997).[4] Such a result would raise the living standards of workers in developing countries, thereby supporting markets for consumer goods and reducing social tensions caused by inequality (Servais 1989; ICFTU 1996). A social clause would also avoid the possibility of collaboration of Western countries in the exploitation of workers in underdeveloped countries (van Liemt 1989). Finally, a social clause would actually defuse pressures within the Western countries for protectionism by removing one of the main arguments that is used in support of protectionism (van Liemt 1989; ICFTU 1996).

At the global level, the debate over including a social clause in trade agreements notably sharpened at the World Trade Organization (WTO) meeting in Singapore in 1996 and again at the Seattle meeting in 1999 (Charnovitz 1987; van Liemt 1989; Rodrick 1994; Fields 1995; Lee 1997; WTO 1996, 1998; Kahn and Sanger 1999; Srinivasan, 2001). Although the WTO has tried to take the position that matters of international labor standards are the purview of the ILO (WTO 1998), and therefore not a trade issue, the Seattle WTO negotiations were effectively ended because of the intransigence of participants over several issues, one of which was labor standards.

Regionally, the United States, Canada, and Mexico were able to negotiate the North American Free Trade Agreement (NAFTA) only by separating labor standards from the main body of the treatment and negotiating those separately. The basic concern in the United States and Canada during the negotiations was that the lower Mexican wages and labor standards and the geographical proximity of the U.S. and Canadian markets to Mexico would encourage domestic firms to shift existing production to Mexico or to invest in new facilities in Mexico rather than in the United States or Canada. The result in the United States and Canada would be both employment losses and lower wages and benefits, the latter occurring because firms would use the threat of a production shift to obtain wage and benefit concessions from workers. There was also a concern that the U.S. and Canadian governments would be pressured to lower their labor standards to permit firms to compete more easily with Mexican firms or with U.S. and Canadian firms producing in Mexico.

The resulting side agreement, completed after the signing of NAFTA—the North American Agreement on Labor Cooperation (NAALC)—demonstrated the tension between national sovereignty and international harmonization. Under NAALC, shared perceptions of the rights of workers were articulated, while at the same time national sovereignty with respect to labor and employment policy was protected. Each of the signatories agreed to enforce its own labor standards; however, NAALC does not commit any of the three NAFTA signatories to enact any labor or employment laws. Indeed, the agreement provides "full respect for each Party's constitution . . . recognizing the right of each Party to establish its own domestic labor standards, and to adopt or modify accordingly its labor laws and regulations" (Bradsher 1993; Farnsworth 1993; NAALC 1993[5]). Rather, NAALC states that "[e]ach Party shall promote compliance with and effectively enforce its labor law through appropriate government action."[6] This is to be accomplished primarily through publicity and official consultations. NAALC does not dictate standards, and there is no explicit prohibition against statutorily changing labor standards.

In addition, NAALC does not include trade sanctions. Noncompliance with the recommendations of the process will result in an order to comply and a monetary remedy,[7] which must be no greater than 0.7 percent of the volume of trade between the two countries (the complaining country and the country against which the complaint was lodged). The money, paid by the offending government, goes into a fund to enhance the enforcement of labor laws in the offending country.[8]

Despite the failure to achieve an international consensus, several trade agreements that include labor standards have been implemented. In these cases, treaties have allowed for sanctions against labor violations. Worldwide agreements made for tin in 1975 and 1981, cocoa in 1986, sugar in 1987, and natural rubber in 1979 and 1987 all contain provisions that address the observance or enactment of fair labor standards among the signatories (Servais 1989; van Liemt 1989). The parties to the agreements have "endeavored to maintain labour standards" or promised to "seek to insure" fair labor standards in their countries (Servais 1989). The United States has been extremely active in incorporating links between labor standards in trade in agreements to which it is a signatory. Such agreements include the Caribbean Basin Initiative in 1983, the Generalized System of Preferences (GSP) in 1984, the Overseas Private Investment Corporation in 1985, and the Omnibus Trade and Competitiveness Act of 1988 (Servais 1989; van Liemt 1989). As a result of the sanctions incorporated in the GSP legislation, two countries, Nicaragua and Romania, lost GSP status in 1987 (Servais 1989).

The Caribbean Basin Initiative in 1983 and the related Caribbean Basin Economic Recovery Act of 1990 (CBERA) permitted the president of the United States to give preferential trade status to countries in the Caribbean basin, but also permitted the president to deny such preferences to any Caribbean basin country that failed to provide its workers with internationally recognized worker rights (van Liemt 1989; Stamps, Kornis, and Tsao 1996). Although no country has been denied CBERA-related trade benefits as a result of worker rights violations, Guatemala was the subject of a review in 1995 based on a petition filed with the International Trade Commission by the AFL-CIO (Stamps, Kornis, and Tsao 1996; Jennings et al. 1997). That review was terminated on May 2, 1997 (Jennings et al. 1997).

At the national level, in the 1980s, the United States included international worker rights provisions in legislation creating the Overseas Private Investment Council, the GSP, and the Omnibus Trade and Competitiveness Act (van Liemt 1989). Recently, however, issues of worker rights have been raised in two contexts: concerns about international labor conditions in the apparel industry, and presidential "fast track" authorization for trade agreements. Public concerns about labor practices in the apparel industry resulted in the establishment of the Apparel Industry Partnership Agreement in April, 1997 (Branigan 1997; Greenhouse 1997). Under the agreement, which was announced by the U.S. president, several large apparel manufacturers and the unions representing employees in the apparel industry agreed to establish workplace codes of conduct, provide for external monitoring of working conditions, and recruit additional firms.

Despite U.S. participation in treaties that do incorporate labor provisions, however, fear that labor standards may be neglected in future agreements has hampered U.S. participation in trade negotiations. Twice in the last three years, the president has requested fast-track authority from Congress and been turned down. Fast-track authority means that the Executive Branch is delegated the authority to negotiate trade terms that may require changes in domestic law. Congress may include goals for the trade negotiations, but congressional objectives are general and advisory only. The Executive Branch is delegated the authority to enter into international agreements, and writes whatever legislation is necessary to meet the terms of the agreement. Congress retains the right to vote yes or no on whatever agreement the Administration negotiates (Mitchell 1997). Congress declined to grant the president fast-track authority in both 1997 and 1999, in part over concerns that the president would give insufficient consideration to labor (and environmental) issues (Mitchell 1997; Abramson and Greenhouse 1997).

Opposition to a Link Between Trade and Labor Standards

Opposition to direct links between labor standards and trade has arisen on the basis of economic principles, political theory, and practical grounds. The opposition to a social clause from an economic point of view is based on the theory of comparative advantage. The imposition of internationally set labor standards would have the effect of negating the comparative advantage of less-developed countries. If developing countries have a comparative advantage in low-wage, low-skilled labor, then they should produce goods that incorporate relatively large amounts of such labor.

Moreover, focusing solely on legislated standards does not take into account the differences in factor productivity; when productivity is taken into account, true labor cost differentials between countries with "low" and "high" standards decline (Srinivasan 1995; Golub 1997). To create a universal set of labor standards in the presence of a diversity of factor endowments would result in a suboptimal solution for at least one country. An optimal solution would require compensation from the winners to the losers; however, such compensating transfers rarely occur (Fields 1995; Srinivasan, 2001). Although the creation of minimum labor standards *within* a country should properly address internal market failures, according to this perspective there is no justification for *internationally imposed* standards (Srinivasan 1997).

Politically based arguments reject the "morality" notions claimed by those who advocate a social clause. They argue that the attempt to create international labor standards and link them to trade is primarily a protectionist device on the part of developed countries to prevent developing countries from exporting goods (Servais 1989; van Liemt 1989; Srinivasan 1997). Given cross-country differences in income levels, a country may decide it is in its best interest to select a low level of labor standards relative to other countries; that choice is a matter of national sovereignty (Srinivasan 1995, 1997; Brown, Deardorff, and Stern 1997; Basu and Van 1998; Lee 1997). Those who make this argument frequently accuse developed countries of being hypocritical, noting that if attempts to force developing countries to raise labor standards are based on altruism, then those countries advocating such a rise should be willing to make income transfers to the less-developed countries or to support the lifting of restrictions on migration (Srinivasan, 1997). They also point out that the developed OECD countries do not themselves adhere to many of the human rights that the higher labor standards would impose on the less-developed countries (Srinivasan 1997).

Finally, there is a view that labor standards matters are not trade matters (Rodrick 1994) and do not belong in a trade agreement. This perspective appears to be held implicitly rather than explicitly, but it is evidenced by the traditional absence of labor-related provisions in many of the major trade treaties, such as the GATT treaties and the Free Trade Agreement between the United States and Canada. The WTO has taken the official position that labor standards matters should be addressed by the ILO, implicitly endorsing the view that trade and labor issues should be separate (WTO 1998).

More recently, however, there appears to be a willingness to recognize a link between trade and labor standards. One example, already discussed, is the NAFTA side agreement, NAALC. In addition, the social charter is gradually becoming part of the treaties of the European Union (EU). Despite a contentious history, since 1992, the EU Commission has enacted directives (legislation binding on all member states) on works council, sex discrimination, and part-time workers; this legislation was accomplished at the time only through a provision in the Maastricht Treaty that permitted the United Kingdom to opt out of the directive (Springer 1994; European Union 1994, 1998a,b).[9] However, the 1996 Singapore Ministerial Declaration renewed the organization's commitment to observing core labor standards and to cooperation with the ILO (WTO 1996).

INSTITUTIONAL MECHANISMS FOR SETTING AND ENFORCING INTERNATIONAL LABOR STANDARDS

In practice, it has been impossible to obtain an international consensus on linking labor standards to trade agreements or on possible mechanisms for enforcement. It is acknowledged that the interests of developed countries differ from those of less-developed countries; it has been difficult, therefore, to create uniform substantive standards that would apply across all countries (Servais 1989; van Liemt 1989).[10]

The primary international organization charged with protecting worker welfare is the ILO, created in 1919. Part of its mission is to set labor standards. The two vehicles the ILO uses to set labor standards are conventions and recommendations. Conventions are intended to lay down binding obligations, although their adoption is voluntary. Recommendations are intended to serve as guidelines, setting out good practice.

The procedure for establishing conventions and recommendations is for the secretariat of the ILO to carry out the necessary research and prepare reports on the subject concerned, and for the measure proposed to be considered by three groups: the Governing Body, in whom executive authority is vested; a specially appointed independent expert group; and the annual International Labour Conference, which has ultimate decision-making authority. The Governing Body and the Conference are both tripartite bodies. When the Conference approves final wording, usually after a second meeting, conventions and recommendations are communicated to member states, who are asked to present them to the appropriate law-making bodies within a fixed period of time. No country is obliged to adopt them, but once a convention is ratified, it becomes binding until it is repudiated. A country that ratifies a convention is required to report periodically on how it has fulfilled its obligations. Even countries that have not ratified are required to report periodically on their practices related to the convention. The reports are reviewed by the Committee of Experts on the Application of Conventions and Recommendations. When a complaint is made against a country for failing to adhere to a ratified convention or recommendation, the ILO procedures provide for representations by employers and workers' organizations and complaints by other governments. This procedure is based on moral suasion and public information (OECD 1996).

Both the number of conventions and the number of ratifications have gradually risen. As of 1997, the ILO had promulgated 180 conventions and 187 recommendations. Its 174 members had effected 6,431 ratifications. The United States has ratified only 10 conventions, arguing that its federal structure prevents ratification. Other federalist nations, however, have ratified many ILO conventions: 57 in Australia, 29 in Canada, and 96 in France. The country that adheres to the most conventions is Spain (103).

Several features of the procedure undermine the effectiveness of the conventions. To start with, by the time the necessary compromises have been made to finalize the conventions, the ambit and force of the conventions have already been restricted and weakened in the eyes of those who wanted them to be forceful. Further, whether any disregard of the practical implementation of a convention comes to light (if the country concerned fails to invigilate it) depends largely on whether it is brought to the attention of the ILO. Once a complaint is brought, the investigation of the complaint is usually a slow business. In addition, from a practical point of view, the ILO lacks the ability to sanction countries who do not comply, and so is likely to seek to conciliate the parties rather than adopting a condemnatory attitude.

The standard-setting role of the ILO has taken on renewed importance in the debate about a "social clause" in international trade agreements. One of the key problems is that if a trade agreement is conditional on the observance of particular labor standards, it is unclear who is to judge whether a country is abiding by its commitments; bodies dealing with trade have little experience of labor matters, and labor experts are typically unfamiliar with trade. The problems created by this lack of cross-context expertise are compounded by the fact that both trade negotiations and ILO procedures are necessarily slow.

Nevertheless, the existence of the ILO and its conventions, many of which have been ratified by a large number of countries, suggests some broad international consensus (if not unanimity) on basic principles of core worker rights (Lee 1997; ILO 1995). Several proposals are currently circulating to reform aspects of the ILO's complaint investigation and dispute resolution process. The director of the ILO has proposed a joint WTC-ILO body to examine charges of violations of ILO conventions 29, 87, 98, 100, 105, 110, and 138—freedom of association and collective bargaining, prohibitions on forced labor, antidiscrimination, and restrictions on child labor (Maier 1994). To take into account the characteristics of individual countries, he recommended a tripartite process to determine the measures or improvements that could be made toward reaching the goal of compliance with these standards (Maier 1994). Rodrick (1994) has proposed a system of formal public complaints before domestic bodies, such as the United States International Trade Commission. This procedure would require testimony from parties and groups that would be adversely affected by trade restrictions against the respondent company so that the public interest and self-interested motives of the complainant could be determined. And the OECD has raised the possibility of using the WTO trade policy review mechanism to address "social dumping" as a result of low labor standards. The notion is that governments that permit low labor standards are providing an indirect subsidy to producers, permitting them to sell their goods to importing countries at artificially low prices.

THE EMERGENCE OF LABOR STANDARDS ENFORCEMENT IN THE EUROPEAN UNION

The ILO is no longer the only international body establishing international labor standards. The European Union (EU), covering nearly all Western and Southern European countries, has been strengthening its involvement in labor matters, particularly since the mid 1980s. It is important to note some significant differences between European and U.S. approaches to labor standards. Europeans and Americans have held somewhat different views on labor standards and the provision of public welfare since before World War II (although there were differences among European countries too). After the war these differences widened. With an unprecedented 25 years or more of economic growth, labor standards were improved in both Europe and America, but, although European workers expected—and obtained—improvements in wages and working conditions, they also sought improvements in public welfare provision, far more so than did U.S. workers.

In several European countries, that trend can be attributed to the teaching of the Roman Catholic Church on social matters. Politicians on the left and many on the right supported improving protection at work. If not able to build a welfare state that offered protection from the cradle to the grave, they sought to offer at least unemployment benefits, health care, sickness pay, and pensions, most of which were established in advance of such programs in the United States, or at least were more generally applicable among the population. In addition to these social guarantees, unions in many countries achieved greater recognition of workers' rights to workplace consultation, protection against unfair dismissal, and severance pay, strengthened in some cases by representation on boards of directors.

In the immediate aftermath of the war, the United Kingdom took the lead, establishing a comprehensive welfare state, including, for a time, completely free health care. But the country's relatively poor economic performance meant that it was not many years before other countries surpassed its level of social benefits.

Sweden was a particularly interesting innovator. There, more of the improvements stemmed from negotiation between central unions and employers and less from government legislation, as befitted a country with an exceptionally high level of unionization. Since the ruling party through most of the years from 1932 to the present was socialist, there was a generally amicable division of responsibility between government and labor in deciding the form of social advance. A notable example was the creation of Sweden's labour market board, AMS (*Arbetsmarknadsstyrelsen*), a public body virtually managed by employers and unions, which has operated what the Swedes have called an active manpower policy, with more emphasis than in other countries on training, retraining, job finding, and relocation, and less on simply paying out unemployment benefits. Between 1955 and 1992, Swedish unemployment stayed below 4 percent. West Germany, a country defeated and in ruins in 1945, rapidly achieved both economic success and social advance, in what the Germans called a social market economy. The union-employer relationship was relatively cooperative during that period, in part because of government and employer responsiveness to the desire of workers to share in the overall economic prosperity.

It was in that environment that, in 1957, six countries—Belgium, France, Germany, Italy, Luxembourg, and the Netherlands—made the Rome Treaty, setting up what was then called the European Economic Community (EEC), later becoming the European Union (EU). The Rome Treaty had little to say about labor. To summarize, it called for freedom for workers to work anywhere in the Community; it established a "social fund" that could be used to help displaced workers; it required equal pay for equal work for men and women; and it had generalized clauses looking toward harmonizing a range of legislation and practices and gradually raising living standards.

Over its now more than 40 years of life, the EU has extended to embrace most Western and Southern European countries (shortly to be joined by others) and to cover more and more subjects, including a greater range of social policy—a term that in continental Europe covers labor policy. The executive arm of the EU, the Commission, has extended its activity in the labor field, notably since the mid 1980s, arguing that a common market would be effective only if ordinary workers felt that they were an integral part of the enterprise and would gain from it. To accomplish that, the EU had to have a social dimension. In 1989, to that end the Commission fostered a "social charter," which served to launch a series of measures during the 1990s. While many of those dealt with relatively minor matters, others were more significant. Thus, the 1993 directive[11] on working time established rules concerning vacations, maximum working hours, and overtime; and the 1994 directive on European works councils required that substantial multinational enterprises establish union-wide consultative bodies through which workers' representatives would be informed about the management's plans.

The mass of labor legislation that has been produced cannot be attributed solely to the Commission, though, under the treaties, that body has the responsibility for initiating legislation. Legislation can be effected only by the Council of Ministers—that is, the representatives of national governments—either unanimously or through a weighted majority, according to the subject.

One question to be asked is why, at a time when the world trend is toward fewer regulations, Europe is going in the other direction. Part of the answer is that, in fact, its zeal for labor legislation is now diminishing, and the Commission is being reminded of the provision of the

Maastricht Treaty concerning "subsidiarity," meaning that decisions should be made as low down the regulatory ladder as possible while still satisfying the treaty's objectives. In addition, one member country, the United Kingdom, has never favored more labor legislation and has secured the opt-out from certain kinds of measures already referred to. But, despite some of these counterforces, the main answer lies in the disposition of continental European countries toward such legislation, compared with the typical Anglo-Saxon disposition toward more pragmatic approaches.

Still, the signs are that the flood of European legislation has lessened and is lessening. The treaties rule out some subjects, such as "the rights and interests of employed persons"; and others, such as social security and social protection, require unanimity from the Council of Ministers. Some important proposals are still under consideration, including one that would create a right for worker representation on boards of directors and another aimed at requiring all member countries to have legislation binding firms to establish consultative machinery. But it is far from certain that the more ambitious parts of these proposals will come to much. With few exceptions, the existing legislation deals with relatively minor matters rather than imposing intolerable burdens on managements.

CONCLUSIONS

The discussion in this chapter is intended to provide conceptual and institutional frameworks for understanding the role of labor standards in an international economy. What is evident in this overview is the lack of theoretical and empirical consensus on the relationship between labor standards and trade. This ambiguity is mirrored in the political difficulties faced by both the ILO and the EU in implementing universal standards. All of the sections in this chapter lead to the same conclusion—that our knowledge of the relationship between labor standards and economic outcomes is far from complete and that durable political solutions are unlikely until we know more.

Notes

1. See Krugman (1994, Chapter 12) for a discussion of the conditions under which protectionist strategies can be efficient.
2. For example, Dorsey and Walzer (1993) found that for blue-collar workers, a 1 percent increase in workers' compensation costs led to a 1.4 percent decline in wages.
3. Freeman's argument rests heavily on consumer knowledge of the labor standards embodied in the goods they purchase. He provides clear, dramatic examples of consumer willingness to pay for labor standards when goods are produced with, for example, slave labor. Compa (1993) provided additional examples such as with the use of child labor. Rodrick (1994) also cited examples in which information about working conditions affects firm production decisions, suggesting that there is a consumer demand for goods produced with some minimal level of labor standards. However, this model depends heavily on the accurate labeling of the labor standards governing the workplace where the various goods are produced. Questions have been raised, moreover, about incentives to label goods falsely, the definition of "low" labor standards, and methods of determining which countries have sufficiently low labor standards to warrant a label.
4. Although most theories of trade point out that the winners from trade could compensate the losers, such compensation rarely occurs (Fields 1995). Rather, the importing country must find ways to compensate the losers, through such vehicles as trade adjustment assistance.
5. *North American Agreement for Labor Cooperation*, Article 2, <http://www.usite.gov:80/wais/reports/arc/W3058.htm and gopher://cyfer.esueda.gov.70/00/ace/policy/nafta/nafta/labor-co.txt>.
6. NAALC, Article 3.
7. NAALC, Article 39.
8. NAALC, Annex 39.
9. The United Kingdom abandoned its opt-out arrangement in 1997, coincident with the election of Labor Party government (European Union 1998c; Hoge 1997; Barber 1997).
10. This difficulty in obtaining international consensus is reflected in differences among trade unionists. Despite the fact that the International Confederation of Free Trade Unions has come out in favor of linking trade and labor standards (ICFTU 1996), union positions in different countries tend to reflect their separate interests. Thus, while Australian unions favor a linkage between trade privileges and labor standards, Malaysian unions do not (Devadason and Ayadurai 1997; Harcourt 1997).
11. *Directives* are laws approved by the Council of Ministers of the EU—the ruling body; they are binding as to their objective but permit some flexibility in consequent national legislation. *Regulations* are binding on everyone in member countries and require no action by parliaments. European laws have precedence over national laws. If a country fails to meet its obligations under European laws, it

may be taken to the European Court of Justice, whose decision is binding. *Recommendations* are guides, which need not be given legislative effect.

3
Definitions and Criteria

DEFINING LABOR STANDARDS

A necessary first step in comparing labor standards in the United States and Canada is to develop a definition of "labor standards" in terms that can be commonly applied in both countries. We suggest that the key characteristic of a labor standard is that it is applicable to all, or almost all, employers and employees.

For the purpose of this study, labor standards have four common components: 1) in both countries they are created and enforced by governments; 2) they are designed to affect workplace transactions primarily; 3) they are generally comparable between the two countries in purpose and administration, such that a fair comparison can be made; and 4) in both countries they have been or could reasonably be adopted.

Governmentally Created and Enforced

The requirement that the standards included in our analysis be governmentally created and enforced ensures that they apply to all employers and employees, taking into account statutory exceptions. Through legislation, government can be seen as establishing a minimum legally enforceable floor for labor standards. We use the following definition of labor standards:

A *labor standard* is any governmentally established procedure, term, condition of employment, or employer requirement that is designed to protect employees from treatment at the workplace that society considers unfair or unjust. The common element across all standards is that they are *mandatory*—that is, they are imposed and enforced by government. Employer failure to comply with the standards brings legal sanctions upon the employer. This provides the *universal* coverage that is needed. The only exclusions are statutory, and can be accounted for and estimated.

Such standards are generally value laden, because what one person considers unfair, another may consider reasonable. For example, the protection of employees who engage in union activity reflects a value that employees should have the right to bargain collectively with their employer without that right being impaired by employer actions vis-à-vis the employees' jobs. Others may hold that property owners should have the right to exclude persons from their property for any reason whatsoever, and should not be constrained to retain employees who organize against their wishes. Because the standards we use are value laden and governmentally imposed, they are linked to the political process in each country.

We acknowledge that there are other benchmarks for labor practices, such as custom and practice in the locality or industry, the marketplace, and collective bargaining. All three of these sources have inherent disadvantages, primarily the absence of a minimum requirement for all firms. For example, custom and practice in an industry may determine days off for holidays, but the holidays are not mandatory, and there is no way of knowing the percentage of firms that do not abide by the custom or practice. While the marketplace may actually raise the level of compensation above the minimum in a region or industry, markets vary over time and across regions, localities, and industries. Thus, while some labor markets may be in a labor surplus, others may be in a labor deficit. Markets in which there is excess demand for labor may exhibit terms and conditions of employment (often referred to as TCEs) that are above the regulated standard. If economic conditions change, however, then the observed conditions may fall closer to the standard than they were under conditions of excess demand.

The TCEs within a collective bargaining agreement in the United States or Canada do not extend beyond the employees contractually covered by that agreement. Whether or not other employers provide TCEs comparable to those negotiated in the agreement depends on whether those employers are unionized; if so, it all depends upon whether the employer and the union negotiate a comparable agreement, the percentage of nonunion employers that believe there is a union threat if they do not match the unionized TCEs, and the extent to which other employers must provide the union-negotiated TCEs to attract a sufficiently high quality and quantity of labor.

We show examples in which this criterion operates in practice in our analyses of vacations and the exclusion of health care in the United States, both discussed below. We consider the United States as not providing vacations because there is no legal requirement on either the federal or any state level that employees receive vacations, although there is a custom and practice that employees receive vacation pay. Similarly, we exclude health care because there is no legal requirement that employers provide employees with health insurance, although there are equal employment opportunity laws that impose such requirements on employers who choose to provide their employees with health insurance or are required by collective bargaining agreements to do so.

Primarily Affecting Workplace Transactions

The second criterion for inclusion in our study as a standard is that the law or regulation is designed, in both countries, to apply primarily at the workplace or to have its primary effect on workplace transactions. We exclude matters that may link somehow to the workplace or a work relationship but do not have the workplace as their primary focus. The best example of such a matter is health care. As the health care financing system in the United States has evolved, it functions primarily through employer contributions. There is no requirement that employers in the United States provide health care coverage to their employees. Under the "governmentally created and enforced" definition, the United States would appear to have a low standard, because all Canadians are covered by government-provided health care. But the Canadian health care system is not funded or administered through the employment relationship. Rather, the Canadian health care system is financed primarily through the general tax system of federal and provincial personal and corporate taxes (Health Canada 1998). In other words, health care is not a workplace issue in Canada as it is in the United States, and therefore we exclude it from our analysis.

For the same reason, we exclude the U.S. social security system and the comparable programs in Canada (see below). Although they are (at least partly) financed through the employment relationship, their primary purpose is to act as an insurance program for persons who are out of the labor force.

Comparable in Purpose and Administration

The third criterion captures our principle that it is important to limit the comparison to those standards that can be fairly compared. This principle provides a second reason for our excluding from the analysis the public pension systems in the two countries—social security and the related programs in the United States, and old age security and the Canada Pension Plan and related programs in Canada. The system in the United States is fully funded by workplace-based payments (from employer and employee, or self-employed persons) and interest, whereas the system in Canada is funded by a combination of workplace-based payments, interest, and general tax revenues (HRDC 1998a,b). Under our criteria, this difference makes it impossible to compare these two programs.

Adoptable in Both Countries

The fourth—and most important—criterion for including a law or regulation as a labor standard in our analysis is that the law or standard could reasonably be adopted in both countries. Since the purpose of this analysis is ultimately to develop a scoring for and ranking of labor standards in the 63 jurisdictions within the United States and Canada, it would be misleading to "score" a jurisdiction or a country lower than it would otherwise be scored because it did not have a standard or a provision that one would think it could not reasonably adopt.

Analyzing Labor Standards

Labor standards fall into one of two categories: 1) standards that require employers to make monetary payments, either to workers or to a government agency; and 2) standards that place constraints on employer actions vis-à-vis workers. The standards we analyze that require employer payments are minimum wage, overtime, paid time off, unemployment or employment insurance, and workers' compensation. The standards that place constraints on employer actions vis-à-vis employees are collective bargaining, equal employment opportunity or employment equity, unjust discharge, occupational safety and health, and advance notice of plant closings or of large-scale layoffs.[1] All these meet our working definition. All involve some government intervention or regulation of the workplace. All ten are value laden. On the one hand, for example, health and safety regulations are said to impose otherwise unnecessary costs on employers so that the work environment can be modified to ensure health and safety. On the other hand, the regulations are designed to protect the welfare of workers.

Sources of Labor Standards

There are four potential sources of labor standards: the Constitution, enabling legislation (statutes and laws), judicial and administrative decisions (decisions issued by administrative bodies or courts), and administrative regulations. Of these four sources, the one we most frequently cite is the enabling legislation. For most standards, the enabling legislation is the basic source, and it allows for the clearest cross-jurisdiction comparison of the level of protection of employees within a jurisdiction.

Although statutorily generated standards have the force of law, standards provided for in a nation's constitution are more binding. In Canada, protections against employment discrimination (employment equity) have their basis in the human rights provisions of the Canadian Constitution rather than in statutes or law (Kelly 1991). This is important because it means that employment equity rights in Canada cannot be eroded through changes in legislation resulting from a shifting political consensus or through adverse judicial decisions. In the United States, by contrast, where employment discrimination is statutorily based, judicial decisions interpreting the legislation have the potential to narrow employee rights. For example, in 1989 the U.S. Supreme Court overturned previously accepted judicial doctrine by ruling that, for a respondent to make a *prima facie* case of discrimination, he or she was required not only to show that protected classes were underrepresented, but also to identify a specific employment practice that caused the underrepresentation. The Court also ruled that the employer could overcome the *prima facie* case by demonstrating a business justification for the employment practice (Ward's Cove). Although that case, which substantially increased the burden on plaintiffs, was eventually reversed by legislative action (Wolkinson and Block 1996), the case does indicate that standards promulgated by legislation do not have the status of standards based on the Constitution.

Similarly, standards promulgated by legislation are subject to being repealed if the political consensus changes. For example, in 1995 the newly elected Conservative government in Ontario enacted legislation repealing many of the provisions of Ontario labor legislation that were considered favorable to unions (Adams 1995). Other provinces show patterns of frequent changes associated with changes in government (Bruce 1989; Block 1994).

Judicial and administrative decisions are a third source of labor standards. In the United States, with the exception of Montana the protections against unjust dismissal are solely based on judicial decisions. Similarly, a key difference between U.S. and Canadian labor laws is the scope of the bargaining—the range of subjects about which the parties to a collective agreement must bargain. In the United States, judicial and administrative decisions have limited the scope of mandatory bargaining to matters involving terms and conditions of employment (Hardin 1992). On the other hand, in Canada, because of judicial decisions all issues are subject to the bargaining process (Adams 1997).

Finally, a standard could be set through regulations adopted by the agency interpreting and administering a statute. In the absence of precise statutory language governing an issue, or in the absence of a judicial or administrative decision, regulations could in theory serve as the *de facto* standard.

Note

1.   See Compa (1993), Charnovitz (1987), and Piore (1990) for examples of other lists of labor standards.

4

Methods for Comparing
Labor Standards

Under ideal circumstances, to compare labor standards between the United States and Canada one would simply determine which labor standards to analyze, and then examine those for the two countries. There are, however, two difficulties with a simple comparison.

First, different levels of government promulgate labor standards in the two countries. Whereas most labor standards in the United States are generally promulgated at the federal level for all firms that affect interstate commerce, labor standards in Canada are adopted at the provincial level for firms and employees within the province, except for certain industries that are viewed as having a direct effect on interprovincial commerce,[1] which are covered by federal law.[2] For example, collective bargaining is federally regulated in the United States, but both provincially and federally regulated in Canada. The result is that standards are more likely to be federally issued in the United States, but province-based in Canada. Any inventory must take account of the varying levels of government. Accordingly, the analysis depends on the jurisdiction of the enabling legislation.

Second, a primary difference between the U.S. and Canadian governmental structures is that in the United States, if a federal statute governs some aspect of the workplace, the federal rule prevails unless the state standard is higher. In some cases, states will have statutes that appear to allow lower standards, generally because either the state has legislated a lower standard in anticipation of a possible repeal or revision of the federal standard, or the state statute was imposed long ago and never repealed despite its lack of effect. Such state statutory standards apply to classes of workers excluded from federal legislation, typically those that do not affect interstate commerce. In Canada, by contrast, with a few exceptions the federal standard usually applies only to federal government employees and those industries that can reasonably be thought of as involved in interprovincial commerce

(*Canada Labour Code* 1988). Except for employees in those industries, the provincial standards prevail.

As discussed in the preceding chapters, the ultimate goal in this research is to develop a method of comparing labor standards among different jurisdictions, in this case ranking the jurisdictions in the United States and Canada with regard to the 10 labor standards chosen for this study. Such a ranking not only generates a usable summary of the differences among jurisdictions in those labor standards, but also allows researchers to use the rankings to test hypotheses regarding the effect of a jurisdiction's labor standards on various economic phenomena, such as the level of imports and exports.

OUTLINE OF THE METHODS

The ranking of a labor standard can be thought of as involving three components: 1) the substance of the standard as it is specified by its enabling legislation, 2) the rigor with which the statute is enforced, and 3) the extent of the labor force that enjoys its protection. Our method of comparing the labor standards uses four steps: First, we analyze the substance—that is, the statutory provisions—of each of the standards. Second, we derive a method of measuring the nature of enforcement. Third, we develop an index—which we call the basic index—of the strength of the labor standard in a jurisdiction by weighting the various statutory provisions and enforcing efforts for each standard. And finally, we deflate the weighted standards by an estimate of the percentage of the labor force covered by each standard.

To rank the labor standards as they affect the typical employer or worker in a jurisdiction, we calculate the basic index for each labor standard for each subnational jurisdiction (U.S. states and Canadian provinces and territories). To make cross-country comparisons, we generate both an unweighted average for each labor standard for each country as well as one weighted by each subnational jurisdiction's share of its country's employment. In our results, we refer to these as the unweighted and weighted indices.

The fourth step in our method involves deflating the weighted indices derived above by the percentage of the labor force covered by each standard (for standards for which coverage is relevant) to create a measure of the overall employee welfare associated with the labor standard. As such, it provides more of an aggregate, societal-level measure than does the basic index. We call this the deflated index. Because both the basic index and the deflated index present useful and complementary information, we present both.

THE SUBSTANCE OF THE STANDARDS

The primary component of all the indices is the statutory substance of the labor standards. To derive this, we code and array provision categories that are comparable across all jurisdictions. We incorporate the provisions into the analysis as discussed more fully in the later sections in this chapter.[3]

ENFORCEMENT

The second component in our indices is that of enforcement.

Rights of Judicial Appeal: General Considerations

Our focus here is on litigants' rights of judicial appeal outside of the administrative agency that has the primary responsibility for enforcing the statute.[4] This analysis takes the position that the broader the rights of appeal from the decision of the administrative agency, the weaker the enforcement mechanism. This proposition is based on two factors: first, the principle of "justice delayed, justice denied" (Weiler 1983; Block and Wolkinson 1985; Novak and Somerlot 1990; Brudney 1996); and second, the likelihood that an agency charged with administering a standard will be more expert in administering that standard than will a court, and also that it may interpret that standard in a way that is more sensitive to the employee beneficiaries of the statute than the court (the court may see its role as one of interpreting a statute in the context of other, nonstatutory, considerations that may be inconsistent with the employee orientation standards, and it may also not be as expert as the administering agency) (Block and Wolkinson 1985; Crowley 1987; Brudney 1996; Block 1997a). Thus, given good-faith differences regarding the proper interpretation of a statute in a specific set of circumstances, it is more likely that the agency administering the statute will interpret that statute in a manner favorable to the employees than will a court.

If an employer appeals an agency decision finding a violation of a standard, there will be delays in applying the standard. Employers who do not prevail at the administrative agency may maintain their action pending the outcome of the appeal process, thus for a time denying employees that to which they are most likely entitled. An implicit assumption in our enforcement measure is that employers are usually better able than employees to bear the costs of a prolonged dispute over a labor standards violation.

Rights of Judicial Appeal: Comparing the United States and Canada

Comparing the United States and Canada, the literature on appeals of administrative decisions indicates that appeals rights are narrower in Canada than in the United States. Canadian legislation frequently incorporates privative clauses that explicitly limit the power of courts to overturn or review agency decisions.[5] For example, the Ontario Workers' Compensation Act incorporates the following privative clause:

> [t]he order or direction of the Appeals Tribunal or a panel thereof is final and conclusive and not open to question or review in any court upon any grounds and no proceeding by or before the Appeals Tribunal or a panel thereof shall be restrained by injunction, prohibition or other process or procedure in any court or be removable by application for judicial review, or otherwise, into any court.[6]

The language severely limits the extent to which an agency decision in a workers' compensation case can be appealed to the courts.

Compare this language with the appeals language from Section 10(f) of the National Labor Relations Act in the United States:

> Any person aggrieved by a final order of the Board granting or denying in whole or in part the relief sought may obtain a review

of such order in any United States court of appeals in the circuit wherein the unfair labor practice in question was alleged to have been engaged in or wherein such person resides or transacts business, or in the United States Court of Appeals for the District of Columbia . . . [T]he court . . . shall have the . . . jurisdiction to grant to the Board such temporary relief or restraining order as it deems just and proper, and in like manner to make and enter a decree enforcing, modifying, and enforcing as so modified, or setting aside in whole or in part the order of the Board.[7]

It is clear that there is far broader scope of appeal of agency decisions under the U.S. National Labor Relations Act than under the Ontario Workers' Compensation Act.[8]

Privative clauses do not completely prevent the courts from reconsidering agency decisions. Adams (1997) notes that, although all Canadian labor relations statutes contain privative clauses, the labor relations tribunal remains subject to judicial review on one or more of four grounds: 1) the agency lacked jurisdiction over the matter, 2) the appellant was denied natural justice or due process, 3) the agency's decision was clearly in violation of the law or patently unreasonable, or 4) the agency engaged in fraud or collusion. Still, these are narrow grounds for review as compared with the bases of judicial review in the United States. Indeed, there are no legislative standards in the United States for judicial review of administrative agency decisions.[9]

Even in the absence of a privative clause, Canadian courts generally defer to tribunal decision making. Mullan (1993) observed that Canadian courts have generally adopted the established arguments for deference to tribunal decision making. First, there is the argument based on parliamentary sovereignty: the existence of a tribunal reflects the will of the legislature that decisions be made by the tribunal rather than the courts. The courts have an obligation to honor that legislative choice.

A second argument is based on expertise: because the tribunal regularly, and exclusively, deals with matters within its jurisdiction, it can be expected to be more expert in that area than the courts. A third argument is based on efficiency: if the courts become involved in interpreting a statute, the tribunal becomes redundant. In the same vein, a well-known willingness of the courts to defer to the tribunal discourages appeals from parties who do not prevail.

These differences suggest that appeals to the courts are far more likely in the United States than in Canada. Consistent with this proposition, Block (1994) found that, for the period 1976–1990, on average 33 percent of National Labor Relations Board (NLRB) unfair labor cases were closed with a court rather than a board decision. By contrast, only 7.1 percent of Ontario Labour Relations Board cases during the period 1980–1981 to 1991–1992 were closed with a court decision. The percentages were comparable for cases before the British Columbia Industrial Relations Council (5.2 percent) for the period 1988–1991 and the Canada Labour Relations Board (6.4 percent) for the period 1980–1991.

As regards the matter of statutory interpretation, there is evidence to suggest that agencies administering labor and employment laws in the United States are less successful than agencies administering other laws at having their decisions sustained by the courts. Crowley (1987) found that the success rate of "all social agencies" (including the NLRB, the Equal Employment Opportunity Commission [EEOC], and the Occupational Safety and Health Administration [OSHA]) before the U.S. Supreme Court during the period 1975 to 1983 was 68.3 percent, while the success rate of "economic agencies" (such as the Securities and Exchange Commission and the Interstate Commerce Commission) was 79.1 percent. The combined success rate of the NLRB, the EEOC, and the OSHA was only 63.8 percent (they were successful 30 times out of 47).

These results showed that, during that period, the NLRB was successful before the Supreme Court only 65.6 percent of the time. These numbers are somewhat consistent with other estimates of NLRB success before the courts. Block (1997b) found that, during the period July 1995 through June 1996, the NLRB was successful (defined as upheld "in whole or major part") in 64.9 percent of the cases decided by the courts of appeal. Brudney (1996) found that for the period November 1986 through October 1993, the NLRB success rate was 77.1 percent, where success was defined as an NLRB order "wholly enforced or affirmed." For the period October 1989 through September 1996, the NLRB reported that 71 percent of its unfair labor practice orders were fully enforced, and 83 percent were enforced in whole or part (NLRB 1997).[10]

For this research, we are concerned most with the effect of such judicial behavior on labor standards legislation. Our view, based on the foregoing analysis, is that court involvement in the administration of the labor laws generally works to the detriment of worker and labor interests and to the advantage of employer interests. In contrast, the absence of judicial review and the ceding of substantial authority to labor standards agencies works to the advantage of worker and labor interests and to the disadvantage of employer interests.

An analysis of labor standards statutes in the United States reveals no explicit limitations in any statute on court review of agency decisions, in situations where the statute is administered by an administrative agency. This observation along with the foregoing literature review leads us to conclude that there are few constraints on the scope of judicial review of agency decisions in the United States.

Conversely, we observe that there are substantial constraints on judicial review throughout Canada and in all statutes. The Canadian literature reviewed above discusses in some detail the impact of privative clauses, and there is literature indicating that the narrow scope of review extends to situations in which no privative clause exists. We have come across no literature that suggests that the scope of judicial review in Canada is anything other than narrow.

All this suggests that a reasonable coding scheme for judicial review in the two countries is to presume that, for those standards for which judicial review is a relevant consideration, judicial review is broad in the United States (unless the statutory language explicitly indicates otherwise) and narrow in Canada, both in the federal jurisdiction and throughout the provinces (unless the statute indicates otherwise).[11] This is the scheme used in our study.[12]

DEVELOPING THE INDICES

To develop the indices, we first constructed a basic index for each of the labor standards in our study. The basic index for each standard has two parts: a subindex value for each of the standard's provisions, which is larger the greater the level of protection given to employees; and a weight given to each provision within each standard. For the purpose of constructing an index, we treat enforcement mechanisms as additional provisions.

Using a technique developed for coding the provisions in collective bargaining agreements (Kochan and Block 1977; Block 1978a and 1978b),[13] we constructed an ordinal scale for each provision. We assigned subindex values to each relevant statutory provision or enforcement mechanism by giving a value 0 to the absence of a provision, and a value of 10 to the strongest provision. Provisions of intermediate strength received intermediate values in accordance with the number of possible categories in the provision.

Generally,

s_{pdj} = the subindex value assigned to provision p in standard d in jurisdiction j,

where $0 \le s_{pdj} \le 10$.

Although the coding schemes for each of the provisions are discussed below, an example here will illustrate. For collective bargaining laws, jurisdictions in which union recognition can be obtained without an election are assigned a subindex value of 10, and jurisdictions in which an election is required are assigned a value of 0. Thus, for this labor standard provision, there are no intermediate subindex values. In contrast, advance notice requirements for plant closings or large-scale layoffs is an example of a provision that requires an intermediate coding. If the provision of the statute in the jurisdiction requires advance notice of greater than or equal to 16 weeks, the jurisdiction is coded as a 10. Notice of 12 to 16 weeks is coded as 7.5; notice of 8 to 12 weeks is coded as 5.0; notice of 4 to 8 weeks is coded as 2.5; and no provision of notice is coded as 0.

In addition to coding each provision, we established a weighting scheme for provisions within a labor standard, such that the total weights of all the provisions within a standard is equal to 1. Within each standard, greater weights are given to the provisions deemed to be most important. For example, in the minimum wage standard, the level of the minimum wage is weighted at 0.92; the availability of a subminimum (or learner) wage is weighted at 0.04; the possibility of a fine or imprisonment is weighted at 0.02; and the right of appeal is weighted at 0.02. Later in this chapter, we present the different weights and subindex values assigned to each provision within a standard.[14]

w_{pdj} = the weight assigned to provision p in standard d in jurisdiction j,

where $0 \le w_{pdj} \le 1$

Then, the basic index score, X_{dj}, for standard d for jurisdiction j is:

$$X_{dj} = \sum^{n} s_{pdj}\, w_{pdj}$$

where the index consists of n provisions.

ESTIMATING COVERAGE

The final component in the full index is the extent to which the labor force is covered by each labor standard. The justification for including coverage is that the proportion of the workforce that is intended to enjoy the protection afforded by any given labor standard is one component of that standard's effect. Coverage is measured as the proportion of the workforce covered by each labor standard. If coverage is comprehensive—that is, if all workers within a jurisdiction are covered by a particular labor standard—that proportion is equal to 1. What we refer to as the "coverage-deflated" (or simply the "deflated") index is constructed by multiplying the basic index by the coverage proportion. The employment-weighted deflated index is constructed by multiplying the employment-weighted index by the coverage proportion. The incorporation of coverage lowers the indices to the extent that coverage is less than comprehensive.

Coverage criteria are specified in the enabling legislation for each standard. For the 10 standards, there are three bases for coverage criteria: characteristics of the workforce, firm size, and occupation or industry.

Standards Assumed to Have Comprehensive Coverage

For 6 of the 10 standards—protection from unjust discharge, paid time off, antidiscrimination or employment equity, unemployment or employment insurance (UI/EI), health and safety, and advance notice—we assume coverage to be comprehensive (thus equal to 1 for each). Two standards have universal coverage in both the United States[15] and Canada (protection from unjust discharge and paid time off[16]), and we thus set coverage equal to 1 for those two. Antidiscrimination or employment equity laws protect certain classes of individuals from discrimination, for example against race or gender. Because of the difficulty of observing several of the coverage classifications—specifically disability, religion, national origin, and (in Canada) political beliefs—we determined that we cannot generate useful coverage estimates for such laws, and thus for the purpose of constructing the deflated indices we assume coverage also to be equal to 1. It should be recognized, however, that this assumption biases the index upward, although it does not change the rankings across jurisdictions. Finally, coverage for three of the standards—UI/EI, health and safety, and advance notice—is based primarily on firm size. In most cases, any statutory exclusions are for very small firms, and the necessary firm size data were not available. As a result, we again assume coverage to be comprehensive.

Standards Assumed to Have Less than Comprehensive Coverage

Coverage estimates for the four remaining standards—minimum wage, workers' compensation, overtime pay, and collective bargaining—were generated using data from two sources, the Current Population Survey (CPS) for the United States and unpublished data from the Survey of Employment, Payrolls, and Hours for Canada, both for 1993. The CPS data used here are from the March 1993 survey. The CPS sample, composed of households, includes data at the household and individual levels. Individual records were read and aggregated to construct the coverage estimates used in this study. Annual average employment and union membership data from the monthly Canadian employment survey were provided to us at the three-digit Canadian 1980 Standard Industrial Classification (SIC) level in tabular form for all of Canada and by province from the Labour Division of Statistics Canada.[17]

We estimated coverage for the next three standards—minimum wage, workers' compensation, and overtime pay—in the following three steps:

Step 1: Ratio of occupation to industry. For the most part, coverage exclusions for these three labor standards are based on occupation and occasionally industry. Therefore, to estimate the share of the excluded occupations in each jurisdiction, we calculated the share of employment in excluded occupations by major industry sector. Because occupational information is available only for the United States and not for any individual jurisdictions, we assumed that the occupational mix for any given industry, using an abridged version of the one-digit SIC, is constant across jurisdictions and is equal to the occupation-industry ratio for the total United States. For example, we assumed that taxi drivers (excluded from workers' compensation in some jurisdictions) compose an equal share of employment in the manufacturing industry regardless of jurisdiction, and that the share is equal to the U.S. national share of taxi drivers in manufacturing. Summing these ratios over exempted occupational categories and industry yields the total share of exempted employment in the United States, EEMPUS:

$$\text{EEMPUS} = \sum_{ij} (\text{EXOCC}_{ij}/\text{IND}_j)$$

where EXOCC_{ij} is the total employment in the exempted occupational category i in industry j, and IND_j is the total employment in industry j.

The assumption that ratios of occupation to industry are constant across jurisdictions is equivalent to assuming that production functions, at least with respect to their use of labor, do not vary spatially. Clearly, the more homogeneous the industry category, the easier this assumption is to defend. Making this assumption at the one-digit SIC level is necessary in order to keep the estimation process tractable. However, in most cases, the occupations that are excluded from labor standard coverage tend to be clustered in nonmanufacturing, and often in business and personal services. Therefore, we calculated the occupation to industry ratio at the more disaggregate level for the services industry. The resulting abridged industry classification thus includes the following 13 industries: agriculture, forestry, and fisheries; mining; construction; manufacturing; transportation, communication and other public utilities; wholesale trade; retail trade; finance, insurance, and real estate; business and repair services; personal services; entertainment and recreation services; professional and related services; and

NEC (not elsewhere classified). This study is limited to the private sector; all government sectors are excluded.

Step 2: Jurisdictional industry weights. The next step was to calculate the industry mix by industry for each state and Canadian province or territory. The jurisdictional industry weights are simply the proportion of employment in each industry for each jurisdiction. For the United States, we did this by summing individual records from the CPS by industry. For Canada, we aggregated the three-digit provincial employment information into our industry classification scheme. These weights sum to 1:

$$\sum_{j} (EMP_{jk}/EMP_k) = 1$$

where EMP_{jk} is the total employment in sector j in jurisdiction k, and EMP_k is the total jurisdiction employment.

Step 3: Exempted share of employment by jurisdiction. The total share of exempted employment in each jurisdiction, $EXSH_K$ is:

$$EXSH_k = \sum_{ij} (EXOCC_i/IND_j) \times (EMP_{jk}/EMP_k) \times D_{ik}$$

where the first two terms on the right are as previously defined and D_{ik} is a dummy variable that equals 1 if occupation i is exempt in jurisdiction k and 0 otherwise.

An example of the calculation will be instructive and is illustrated in Figure 4.1. Take the taxi driver example discussed previously and apply it to a sample jurisdiction. Assume that taxi drivers constitute 1 percent of manufacturing employment in the United States, that manufacturing accounts for 20 percent of total employment in that jurisdiction, and that taxi drivers are not covered (are excluded from) the relevant labor standard in the jurisdiction. Under these assumptions, the decline in coverage of the relevant labor standard in the jurisdiction accounted for by the exclusion of taxi drivers in manufacturing would be 0.002, which would be the exempted share.

The figure also makes the assumption that the hypothetical occupation servers and buspersons constitutes 2 percent of employment in manufacturing in the United States. This would result in an exempted share of 0.004 resulting from buspersons and servers in manufacturing. On the other hand, if truck drivers constituted 5 percent of manufactur-

Figure 4.1 Example Calculation of Exempted Share

Occupation	(1) Percent employment in manufacturing in jurisdiction	(2) Mfg. as a percentage of total employment in jurisdiction	(3) Excluded in jurisdiction	(4) Excluded occupational share in jurisdiction (1) * (2) * (3)
Taxi drivers	1	20	Yes = 1	0.002
Servers and buspersons	2	20	Yes = 1	0.004
Truck drivers	5	20	No = 0	0

ing employment in the United States, the exempted share would be 0, because truck drivers are covered by the legislation. Thus, the total exempt share from these three occupation-industry combinations is 0.006.

By summing across all excluded occupations in manufacturing in jurisdiction k for any labor standard, we would obtain an exempt share of employment in manufacturing in jurisdiction k for that standard. By making similar calculations for each occupation in each industry, we would obtain an exempt share for each industry in jurisdiction k for that standard. Summing all the exemptions in all industries would provide an exempt share of employees in jurisdiction k for that standard.

Our procedure allows for two sources of coverage variation. The first is difference across jurisdictional statute—that is, whether D_{ik} equals 0 or 1. The other is industry mix, which will differentially weight each occupation's share of the total employment in each jurisdiction.

For the final standard, collective bargaining, we estimated coverage using the same logic with two slight variations. In some cases, under a collective bargaining law, there might be variation within certain occupations in the right to organize and thus in coverage. For example, some professionals may also be managers or supervisors and are not covered by the National Labor Relations Act.[18] To account for this, we assigned a weight of 0.5 to those occupational categories for the purpose of counting them in calculating the ratio of exempt occupation to industry. The second variation was to make the simplifying assumption that all jurisdictional exclusions were the same as those specified in the U.S. National Labor Relations Act. We made this assumption for computational reasons, and it will tend to overstate the coverage in most Canadian jurisdictions. As a result of this assumption, all variation in coverage across jurisdictions is a function of industry mix.

MODEL FOR COMPARING LABOR STANDARDS

As discussed in Chapter 3, labor standards fall into two basic categories: standards requiring direct employer payments, either to employees or to government, and standards constraining the employer's behavior vis-à-vis its employees. For the standards requiring employer payments, the provisions considered are the level of required payments, the extent of exclusions, and the severity of penalties for statutory violations. In general, the required payment level is given the highest weight, and the higher the received payment, the higher the standard. For the standards constraining employer behavior, the provisions considered depended on the purpose of the standard, but broadly include the breadth of the constraints on employers, the amount of freedom given to employees, and the penalties on the employer. The greater the constraints on the employer or the greater the employee freedom, the higher the standard.

THE LABOR STANDARDS ANALYZED: PROVISIONS, WEIGHTS, AND SCORES[19]

This section of the chapter describes the statutory provisions, the weighting scheme, and the scoring (subindex values) for each standard. The section starts with the standards requiring employer payment, followed by the discussion of standards constraining employer actions at the workplace.

Standards Requiring Employer Payment

Minimum Wage

The provisions, weights, and subindex values that constitute the minimum wage index are shown in Table 4.1. The basic principle behind the minimum wage is the creation of a wage floor for all employees. Through the enactment of a minimum wage, the government says implicitly that private contracts for a wage below the minimum are undesirable and will not be permitted. On this basis, we give the greatest weight, 0.92, to the level of the minimum wage. We also, however, take into account the fact that in some jurisdictions learners and inexperienced employees are allowed to receive a subminimum wage. This is a modification of the "undesirable contract" notion, but it would apply only to a limited number of employees and for a limited time, therefore we assign it only a small weight of 0.04. We did not wish to make the appeals and enforcement aspects of the standard greater than the modification of the substantive standard. Thus, each of these is assigned a weight of 0.02.

Overtime

The provisions, weights, and subindex values that constitute the overtime index are shown in Table 4.2. A jurisdiction creates a standard work week, in essence stating that the standard is the amount of time employees are expected to work in a week. The creation of a standard work week, in turn, is based on the notion that employees are entitled to some time during a week for leisure and to attend to personal business. In most cases, hours worked over and above the standard work week are associated with premium compensation for the employees over and above what they would ordinarily earn for those hours, and additional cost for the employer, over and above what the employer would ordinarily pay.

The two key components of an overtime standard are the overtime premium, or multiplier, and the number of weekly hours of work at which the overtime premium requirement is triggered. The greater the overtime premium, and the fewer the number of weekly hours at which the premium is triggered, the more favorable the standard to employees. Some Canadian jurisdictions require the overtime premium paid to

**Table 4.1 Minimum Wage Index: Provisions, Weights, and Subindex
Values**

Provision	Weight	Subindex value
Minimum wage level (12/20/98)	0.92	
≥ US$5.75 or $C8.05		10
US$5.50–$5.74 or $C7.70–$8.04		9
US$5.25–$5.40 or $C7.35–$7.69		8
US$5.00–$5.24 or $C7.00–$7.34		7
US$4.75–$4.99 or $C6.65–$6.99		6
US$4.50–$4.74 or $C6.30–$6.64		5
US$4.25–$4.49 or $C5.95–$6.29		4
US$4.00–$4.24 or $C5.60–$5.94		3
US$3.75–$3.99 or $C5.25–$5.59		2
US$3.50–$3.74 or $C4.90–$5.24		1
Subminimum wage	0.04	
If jurisdiction has no subminimum or if subminimum wage would reduce wage paid below federal or jurisdictional minimum, whichever is higher		10
Otherwise		0
Fines, imprisonment	0.02	
If fines or imprisonment a possible sanction on violator		10
Otherwise		0
Right of appeal of agency decision	0.02	
Yes		10
No		0

Table 4.2 Overtime: Provisions, Weights, and Subindex Values

Provision	Weight	Subindex value
Overtime	0.95	
1.5 × reg rate after 40 hours per week		10
2 × reg rate after 48 hours per week		8.57
1.5 × reg rate after 44 hours per week		7.14
1.5 × reg rate after 48 hours per week		5.71
1.5 × min wage after 40 hours per week		4.18
1.5 × min wage after 44 hours per week		2.85
1.5 × min wage after 48 hours per week		1.42
Limits on rights of appeal of agency decisions	0.05	
Yes		10
No		0

be a multiple of the jurisdiction's minimum wage rather than the employee's wage. This is also taken into account in our coding.

It should be noticed that the highest subindex value is assigned to provisions in which the employer is required to pay 1.5 times the hourly rate after 40 hours. This is assigned a higher score than a standard that requires 2 times the hourly rate after 48 hours. Data on average hours worked justify this scoring. Between 1988 and 1997, the average weekly hours for U.S. production workers never exceeded 41.5 in any single month (U.S. Department of Labor 1998). For Canada in 1997, the average weekly hours worked for employees in mining, quarrying, and oil wells—the industry group with the highest average weekly hours—was 42.5 (Statistics Canada 1998). Therefore, it seems reasonable to presume that most overtime is assigned in hours 41 to 48, and that statutes that give employees overtime at lower hours, albeit at a lower rate, are more favorable to employees than are statutes that give employees overtime only after more hours even if at a higher rate.

Paid Time Off

The provisions, weights, and subindex values that constitute the paid time off index are shown in Table 4.3. The principle underlying this index is that the greater the level of paid leisure time to which employees are entitled, the higher the standard.

We focused on two types of paid time off that would be universally available to all employees regardless of random occurrences, such as

Table 4.3 Paid Time Off: Provisions, Weights, and Subindex Values

Provision	Weight	Subindex value
Holidays	0.165	
13 or more days		10
12–12.9 days		7.8
11–11.9 days		6.7
9–9.9 days		5.6
8–8.9 days		4.4
7–7.9 days		0.3
6–6.9 days		0.2
5–5.9 days		0.1
<5 days		0
Pay for overtime	0.335	
Employees must be paid for holidays taken or granted overtime for holidays worked		10
Otherwise		0
Vacation length and pay	0.45	
3 weeks vacation at 6% of pay or reg. pay		10
2 weeks vacation at 6% of pay		6.67
2 weeks vacation at 4% of pay or reg. pay		3.33
No vacation, no pay		0
Eligibility for vacation pay	0.05	
After 10 months service		10
After 12 months service		6.67
After more than 12 months service		3.33
No provision		0

illness or bereavement. These two types are holidays and paid vacations. Half of the weight of the index—that is, 0.5—is associated with
holidays. Within the holiday component, one-third (0.165) is assigned
to the number of holidays, and two-thirds (0.335) to provisions for pay
or overtime for holidays worked. A required holiday standard is coded
as higher when it is paid or requires overtime pay than when it does
not.

The vacation component (0.5) of the index also comprises two subcomponents. We give 90 percent of the vacation component (0.45) to
the amount of paid vacation to which the employee is entitled. The
smaller subcomponent (0.05) is the length of service that determines
eligibility for vacation pay; this subcomponent is assigned a smaller
weight because these standards generally make employees eligible
after a year of tenure or less with the employer. Therefore, most
employees under such statutes are eligible for vacation pay, and eligibility is not a source of great variation among firms.

Unemployment or Employment Insurance

The provisions, weights, and scores that constitute the UI/EI index
are shown in Table 4.4. In general, UI/EI systems are designed to provide financial support to employees during periods of unemployment
that are the result of factors beyond their control. The systems consist
of a tax-based financing mechanism and a benefit structure. In general,
the higher the level of benefits and the greater the length of time
employees may receive benefits, the higher the standards. In addition,
the standard is also considered to be higher the greater the percentage
of the financing borne by the employer, and lower to the extent that the
employee must bear a portion of the tax burden.[20]

As Table 4.4 shows, the greatest weight goes to the level of the
average weekly benefit as a percentage of the average weekly wage.
This is based on the notion that the greater the replacement of the
employee's regular wage, the higher the standards. The subcomponent
assigned the second greatest weight is the employee's UI/EI tax rate.
The higher the employee's tax, the lower the subindex value assigned,
because any employee payment is seen as offsetting the benefits. The
principle is that if employees must pay part of their wages into the fund
each pay period, that payment can be viewed as offsetting what they
would receive if they were unemployed. Further, employees who are

**Table 4.4 Unemployment or Employment Insurance: Provisions,
Weights, and Subindex Values**

Provision	Weight	Subindex value
Taxable wage base	0.1	
≥ U.S.$30,000/Can.$41,100		10
U.S.$25,000–U.S.$29,999/Can.$34,250–Can.$41,099		8.3
U.S.$20,000–U.S.$24,999/Can.$27,400–Can.$34,249		6.7
U.S.$15,000–U.S.$19,999/Can.$20,500–Can.$27,399		5.0
U.S.$10,000–U.S.$14,999/Can.$13,700–Can.$20,499		3.3
U.S.$5,000–U.S.$9,999/Can.$6850–Can.$13,699		1.7
Employee tax rate	0.3	
No employee tax		10
> 0 but < 1%		8.3
1–2%		6.7
2–3%		5.0
3–4%		3.3
4–5%		1.7
Average weekly benefit[a]	0.35	
45–49%		8.3
40–44%		6.7
35–39%		5.0
30–34%		3.3
< 30%		1.7
Maximum total benefit[b]	0.25	
45 weeks		10
43 weeks		7.5
39 weeks		5.0
26 weeks		2.5

[a] As a percent of average weekly wage.
[b] It is assumed that all employees are entitled to 13 weeks of federal extended UI/EI benefits.

not laid off do not receive benefits but do pay part of the premium. The subindex is coded higher the lower the tax rate; lower tax rates mean lower payments for employees.

Weighted at 0.25 is the length of time that employees may receive benefits. The greater the length of time, the higher the standard. This subcomponent is assigned a slightly lower rate than the benefit level and the tax rate because not all employees will be required to draw benefits for the maximum period. The smallest subcomponent, weighted at 0.1, is the taxable wage base. The higher the wage base, the greater the financial resources of the fund from which benefits are drawn.

Workers' Compensation

The provisions, weights, and subindex values used to develop a workers' compensation index are shown in Table 4.5. The criteria used represent the essential program dimensions of the state and provincial workers' compensation systems based on the 19 essential recommendations from the *Report of the National Commission on State Workmen's Compensation Laws* (1972). The recommendations are broken into categories that reflect different aspects of the law. In particular, eight refer to the extent of coverage, nine refer to the adequacy of income benefits, and two refer to the scope and adequacy of medical benefits. Data on compliance across the states are compiled annually by the Employment Standards Administration within the U.S. Department of Labor. The data used to construct the index in the Chapter 5 appendix come from the 1997 report (U.S. Department of Labor 1997) and a reprint of its 1995 report in the *1996 Workers' Compensation Yearbook* (Burton and Schmidle 1996). The Burton and Schmidle source was one of two used to derive compliance among the Canadian jurisdictions. The other source was the *1996 Analysis of Workers' Compensation Laws* (U.S. Chamber of Commerce 1996).

With the exception of the right to file across jurisdictions—the one recommendation for which we could not obtain reliable data for the Canadian jurisdictions—the essential recommendations are weighted equally. Two of the recommendations, compulsory coverage, and death benefits for family members, are themselves subdivided into parts. Those for compulsory coverage are weighted equally. Among the four parts to the family death benefits one (continuation of death benefits to

Table 4.5 Workers' Compensation: Provisions, Weights, and Subindex Values

Provision	Recommendation number[a]	Weight	Subindex value[b]
Program dimensions			
Compulsory coverage	(2.1)		
Compulsory coverage for private employment	(2.1a)	0.024	10
No waivers permitted	(2.1b)	0.024	10
No exemption based on firm size	(2.2)	0.047	10
Farmworkers covered	(2.4)	0.047	10
Casual and household workers covered	(2.5)	0.047	10
Mandatory government worker coverage	(2.6)	0.047	10
No exemptions based on employee class	(2.7)	0.047	10
Employee choice over where to file	(2.11)	0.000	10
Coverage for all work-related diseases	(2.13)	0.047	10
Temporary, total disabilities (TTD) benefits ≥ 66 2/3% of wages (subject to maximum)	(3.7)	0.047	10
Maximum TTD benefit at least 100% standard average weekly wage (SAWW)	(3.8)	0.047	10
Retain prevailing part-time (PT) definition	(3.11)	0.047	10
PT benefits ≥ 66 2/3% of wages (subject to maximum)	(3.12)	0.047	10
Maximum PT benefit at least 100% SAWW	(3.15)	0.047	10
Benefit duration = disability duration	(3.17)	0.047	10
Death benefits ≥ 66 2/3% of wages	(3.21)	0.047	10
Maximum death benefit at least 100% SAWW	(3.23)	0.04	10
Family death benefits	(3.25)		10
Benefits to widow(er)	(3.25a)	0.024	10
Lump sum to widow(er) on remarriage	(3.25b)	0.008	10

Provision	Recommendation number[a]	Weight	Subindex value[b]
Benefits to dependent child until 18	(3.25c)	0.008	10
Benefits to dependent child until 25 if student	(3.25d)	0.008	10
No statutory $ limit on medical or rehab. services	(4.2)	0.047	10
No time limit on right to medical or rehab. services	(4.4)	0.047	10
Right of appeal			
Agency		0.05	10
Internal process		0.05	10
Levels of appeal available		0.05	
No appeal beyond internal process			10
Option to go to State Court or Supreme Court			7.5
May go to State Court and Supreme Court			5.0
No internal process but may go to State Court or Supreme Court			2.5
No internal process but option to go to State Court and Supreme Court			0

[a] Recommendations as presented in Report From National Commission (1972).
[b] For provisions that have no subindex values listed, jurisdiction is given a subindex value of 10 if its law is in full compliance with the recommendation or 0 otherwise.

the spouse) is weighted three times as heavily (0.024) as the remaining three (a lump sum to the spouse upon remarriage, benefits to children until age 18, and benefits to children until age 25 if in school), each weighted at 0.008. The logic behind this weighting scheme is that benefits to the spouse compensate for the loss of a breadwinner, and are thus the primary purpose of survivor benefits. Children will benefit through these surviving spouse benefits or be financially cared for if that spouse remarries.

The measures of enforcement for this standard are based on the principle articulated earlier, that justice delayed is justice denied. Disputes are relatively common in workers' compensation cases, and the jurisdictions vary considerably in the structure used to resolve disputes, including the presence of pretrial hearings, mediation, and provisions for alternative dispute resolution. The research on the value of the pre-formal-hearing process is mixed, indicating that in some cases it resolves disputes earlier but in others prolongs them (Ballantyne and Mazingo 1999), thus making it difficult to characterize the enforcement properties of this stage of dispute resolution. For that reason, we consider only the features of the formal structure in developing the enforcement component of the index. Three features are included: the presence of an internal, administrative, first-level formal hearing; the presence of an internal appeals process; and the number of levels of appeal after the internal appeal process is exhausted. We base this on the principle described earlier, that an internal agency will be more likely to be knowledgeable about the purpose of the statute and to make decisions that favor that purpose. Thus, the presence of an internal dispute resolution process is given a score of 10; the absence of such a process is scored 0 (in that case, disputes are resolved by trial in state court). Using the same logic, the presence of an internal appeals agency is coded the same way: 10 if there is an internal appeals agency; 0 if the decision must be appealed in the judicial system. The third characteristic, the number of levels of appeal beyond the first, is coded such that the fewer the number of possible appeals levels, the higher the score. The possible levels and their attendant scores are: no appeal beyond the internal appeal process (10); after an internal process, can go either to state courts or to the state Supreme Court, but not both (7.5); after internal process, can go to state courts and then to Supreme Court (5); no internal process, but can appeal the administrative decision at either the state court level or the state Supreme Court, but not both (2.5); and, no internal process but can appeal the administrative decision at the state court level and then to the state Supreme Court (0).[21]

Standards Constraining Employer Allocation of Labor

Collective Bargaining

The provisions and weights that constitute the collective bargaining index are shown in Table 4.6. To distill the important components of detailed and complex collective bargaining legislation in both coun-

Table 4.6 Collective Bargaining: Provisions, Weights, and Subindex Values[a]

Provision	Weight
Statutory protection for collective bargaining	0.15
Election not required[b]	0.20
Unlimited subjects of bargaining	0.10
Conciliation rights[c]	0.20
Striker permanent replacements prohibited	0.10
First-agreement arbitration available	0.10
Limits on rights of loser to appeal	0.15

[a] The jurisdiction's subindex value is coded as 10 if the provision is in effect; 0 otherwise.

[b] Election is not required if there is evidence that a majority support the union.

[c] Conciliation during negotiations is compulsory at the request of government or at the request of either party.

tries, we attempted to incorporate those aspects of the law that are at the heart of rights to bargain collectively. These incorporate a statute providing the basic rights, the right to select representation, and the right to negotiate an agreement, when and if a representative is selected. Because all of the provisions in the collective bargaining index were such that a jurisdiction either had the provision, or the jurisdiction did not have the provision, there were no intermediate values for the subindex; the value was 10 if the jurisdiction had a provision, and 2 if it did not.

The two greatest weights, each 0.20, are assigned to the requirement of an election and the right to request conciliation or mediation during negotiations. An election requirement favors employers, resulting in a subindex value of zero, because it gives the employer the opportunity to influence the outcome of the representation process (Weiler 1983). Card checks, on the other hand, the most common method for determining representation in the absence of an election, favor unions because the union has the opportunity to establish representation with no employer involvement (Block 1994).[22]

A mediation or conciliation requirement is also assigned a weight of 0.20 because of the notion that government involvement in the bargaining process makes it more difficult than otherwise for the employer to use its bargaining power to weaken or eliminate the union (Block 1994). Thus, a subindex value of 10 is assigned to jurisdictions where either side can trigger mandatory third-party involvement, and zero is assigned to jurisdictions where there is no mandatory third-party involvement.

Limits on appeal rights are assigned a weight of 0.15, far higher than the weight such limits are assigned in the other indices in which an appeal is relevant. This assignment is based on the literature, which suggests that appeals can be used by employers to maintain a status quo favorable to themselves, that such tactics can be an integral component of employers' legal strategies under the labor laws, and that appeals can be successful for employers in influencing interpretations of the law (Block and Wolkinson 1985; *Report and Recommendations* 1994; Block 1994, 1997a, 1997b; Brudney 1996). Broad rights of appeal are presumed to benefit employers: because most unfair labor practice charges are filed against employers, thus they generally benefit the most from maintaining the status quo. Accordingly, the greater the scope of the appeal rights, the lower the standard.

Weights of 0.1 are assigned to prohibition on striker replacement, the presence of first agreement arbitration, and the absence of limits on the subjects of bargaining. If employer and union preferences are indicated by the political debate, then the ability to replace strikers enhances employer interests, and the absence of that ability enhances union interests (Adams 1995, 1997; Schnell and Gramm 1996; Block, Beck, and Kruger 1996; Block 1997a). The presence of first agreement arbitration also enhances the welfare of the union by establishing a first contract for the union, the most difficult contract for a union to secure (Cooke 1985). Finally, limiting the subject matter of bargaining reduces the scope of union activity and creates opportunities for litigation and delay, which tend to favor the employer (Sockell 1986).

Equal Employment Opportunity and Employment Equity (EEO/EE)

The provisions, weights, and subindex values that constitute the index for EEO/EE are shown in Table 4.7. The basic coding principle was to focus on classes of covered employees as determined by statutes or clearly enunciated judicial doctrine (such as regarding sexual harassment as sex discrimination).[23]   Provisions on judicial doctrine covering such matters as burden of proof and liability are excluded because they tend to be either ambiguous or fact-specific, making coding necessarily arbitrary and often inaccurate.[24]

The greatest weight is given to those characteristics of employees that are the core of antidiscrimination, which include visible minorities and women who would also likely be the largest protected groups. Thus race and gender are each assigned a score of 0.15. The next highest weights, 0.10, are assigned to national origin, age, religion, and disability.   Each of these categories is often specifically covered by statute. Sexual orientation and political beliefs were coded at 0.05 because they are likely less obvious than some of the other protected

Table 4.7 Equal Employment Opportunity and Employment Equity: Provisions, Weights, and Subindex Values

Provision	Weight	Subindex value[a]
Race, visible minorities, Aboriginal peoples	0.15	
Gender	0.15	
National origin or ancestry	0.10	
Religion	0.10	
Age	0.10	
No exceptions		10
Retirement plan exceptions		5
Age not covered		0
Sexual preference or orientation	0.05	
Disability	0.10	
Political beliefs, organization memberships	0.05	
Family leave[b]	0.05	
Sexual harassment	0.03	
Equal pay	0.03	
Reasonable accommodation for disabled employees	0.04	
Limits on rights of appeal	0.05	

[a] For provisions that have no subindex values listed, jurisdiction is given a subindex value of 10 if its law is in full compliance with the recommendation or 0 otherwise.

[b] For pregnancy, illness of a family member, or serious health problem—12–17 weeks, unpaid.

classes. The breadth of coverage for family leave is assigned a weight of 0.05 because other types of leave, such as sick leave, personal leave, and vacation, are used more frequently than family leave, which is used relatively infrequently. Sexual harassment, equal pay, and reasonable accommodation are coded separately because they represent special situations that have received either statutory or special judicial attention. But we limited their weights to 0.03, 0.03, and 0.04, respec-

Table 4.8 Unjust Discharge: Provisions, Weights, and Subindex Values

Provision	Weight	Subindex value
Litigation model		
Discharge model prohibited if implicit contract exists	0.05	
Definitive state ruling in favor of exception		10
No court decision		5
Definitive state ruling against exception		0
Handbook exception	0.05	
Definitive state ruling in favor of exception		10
No court decision		5
Definitive state ruling against exception		0
Public policy exception	0.10	
Definitive state ruling in favor of exception		10
No court decision		5
Definitive state ruling against exception		0
Covenant-of-good-faith exception	0.10	
Definitive state ruling in favor of exception		10
No court decision		5
Definitive state ruling against exception		0
Legislative model		
Limited[b]	0.70	10[a]

[a] Coded as 10 if the provision is in effect; 0 otherwise.
[b] Except for misconduct, incompetence, or negligence; limited to "good cause."

tively, because they are also covered under gender discrimination and disability discrimination.

Unjust Dismissal

The provisions, weights, and subindex values that constitute the unjust dismissal index are shown in Table 4.8.   In general, there are two models for protection against unjust dismissal.   The legislative model provides broad-based coverage for all employees, but limits liability for any single incident (St. Antoine 1988; Krueger 1991; Stieber and Block 1992; Wolkinson and Block 1996).   The litigation model does not provide broad coverage, limiting coverage to individual employees who are able to prove that their particular employment contract or work situation is an exception to the employment-at-will standard. Under the litigation model, the existence of an exception for an individual employee must be shown through litigation.   Once shown, however, liability is determined by the judge or jury (Wolkinson and Block 1996).   Given the high cost of initiating litigation, we presume that the legislative model represents a higher standard than the litigation exception model.

Because in principle a jurisdiction could have both legislation and litigation models, we created an index in which the presence of both models would result in a jurisdiction being coded a 10. Because of the broader coverage of the statutory model, we assign jurisdictions with that model a subindex value of 0.70.

In regards to the litigation model, each of the three judicially created exceptions to the employment-at-will doctrine—contractual, public policy (employee may not be discharged if the discharge violates public policy or if employee refuses to commit an illegal act), the covenant of good faith (employer may not discharge an employee to avoid paying monies owed)—was assigned a weight of 0.10 (Wolkinson and Block 1996).   The contractual exception was further subdivided into two parts. States in which courts have ruled that the employee may show a verbal or written contract that he or she would not be discharged except for just cause was coded 0.05. States in which courts have ruled that an employee handbook that states that employees will not be discharged except for just cause constitutes a contract were coded 0.05. Thus, states in which employees may rely on both sources of contract would be coded 0.10.

Within the three judicially created exceptions, a jurisdiction could receive three subindex values: 10 if there is a judicially created exception in the jurisdiction, 0 if a court in the jurisdiction has explicitly ruled that the exception does not exist in that jurisdiction, and 5 if there has been no definitive ruling in the jurisdiction. This middle value is based on the view that the absence of a judicial decision creates legal uncertainty in the jurisdiction: it is unclear whether an exception exists.

Therefore, a jurisdiction with all three judicially created exceptions but with no statutory coverage would receive a subindex of 3.0. A jurisdiction with broad-based coverage but with limited liability would receive a subindex of 7.0. Given what we perceive as revealed employer preferences for the litigation model, we believe this difference is reasonable.[25]

Occupational Safety and Health

The provisions, weights, and subindex values that constitute the occupational safety and health index are shown in Table 4.9. In general, they are based on Wolkinson and Block (1996) and incorporate penalties and required procedures. In the absence of substantial evidence that any single provision is of greatest importance in improving occupational safety and health, all provisions are weighted equally. Although some evidence suggests that the presence of a plant-level committee is important in assuring compliance (Weil 1995), the ultimate responsibility for compliance and penalties still rests with government agencies.

An additional caveat is associated with occupational safety and health standards. The federal government and various state agencies have developed industry- and product-specific occupational health and safety standards that would be impossible to incorporate in an index such as this. To do so would require both an analysis of the industry mix in each jurisdiction and an analysis of the rigorousness of the standards for each industry or product relative to some unknown benchmark.

Table 4.9 Occupational Safety and Health: Provisions, Weights, and Subindex Values

Provision	Weight	Subindex value[a]
Subject to general duty clause	0.02	
Inspection warrant required[b]	0.053	
Maximum penalty for willful violation	0.053	
≥$100,000[c]		10
$80,000–$99,999		8.3
$60,000–$79,000		6.7
$40,000 –$59,999		5.0
$20,000–$39,999		3.3
$1,000 –$19,999		1.7
No penalty		0
Maximum penalty for a serious violation[d]	0.053	
Maximum penalty for a willful repeat violation[d]	0.053	
Repeat violation penalties increased[e]	0.053	
Willful violation causing death[d]		
Penalty for first offense	0.053	
Penalty for second offense	0.053	
Penalty for failing to abate a hazard[f]	0.053	
≥ $10,000[c]		10
$8,000–$9,999		8.3
$6,000–$7,999		6.7
$4,000–$5,999		5.0
$2,000–$3,999		3.3
$1–$1,999		1.7
No fine		0
Reduction in penaltites for firms		
With fewer than 250 employees	0.02	
With written health and safety program	0.02	
With no violations during a specified time	0.02	
Record keeping exemptions for small firms or specified industries	0.02	

(continued)

Table 4.9 (continued)

Provision	Weight	Subindex value[a]
Jurisdiction with stricter standards than federal government	0.053	
Occupational safety committee or represenative required	0.053	
Maximum imprisonment possible	0.053	
24 months		10
12 months		8
6 months		6
3 months		4
1 month		2
Maximum penalty for contravening direction of safety officer or inspector	0.053	
> $100,000[c]		10
$80,000–$99,999		8.3
$60,000–$79,999		6.7
$40,000–$59,999		5.0
$20,000–$39,999		3.3
$1,000–$19,999		1.7
No penalty		0
Maximum penalty for any contravention by anyone[f]	0.053	
Maximum penalty for minor offenses[f]	0.053	
Additional fines possible	0.053	
Penalty for failing to abate a second hazard	0.053	
Limits on appeal of agency decisions	0.052	

[a] For provisions that have no subindex values listed, jurisdiction is given a subindex value of 10 if its law is in full compliance with the recommendation, or 0 otherwise.
[b] Warrant can be demanded before inspector may enter.
[c] All dollar amounts are domestic.
[d] For coding, see column entitled "Maximum penalty for a willful violation of statute" in Wolkinson and Block (1996).
[e] Repeat violation penalties may be increased by a factor of 10.
[f] For coding, see column entitled "Daily penalty assessed for failing to abate a hazard until corrected" in Wolkinson and Block (1996).

Advance Notice of Plant Closings and Large-Scale Layoffs

The provisions, weights, and subindex values that constitute the advance notice index are shown in Table 4.10. The highest provision weights, 0.20, are assigned to provisions on the minimum number of employees necessary for coverage, the amount of advance notice required, whether notice must be given to the affected employees, and whether the employees are entitled to severance pay. The smaller the minimum unit size for coverage, the higher the standard. The longer

Table 4.10 Advance Notice of Plant Closings and Large-Scale Layoffs: Provisions, Weights, and Subindex Values

Provision	Weight	Subindex value[a]
Number of employees for coverage	0.20	
More than 10		10
More than 25		6.7
More than 50		3.3
No provision		0
Maximum time in which layoffs must occur	0.04	
No maximum		10
4–5 weeks		6.7
8 weeks		3.3
No provision		0
Advance notice required	0.20	
> 16 weeks		10
12 to 16 weeks		7.5
8 to 12 weeks		5
4 to 8 weeks		2.5
No notice required		0
Notice to minister of labor or government	0.01	
Notice to affected employee	0.20	
Notice to union	0.10	
Severance pay	0.20	
Limits on appeal of agency decisions	0.05	

[a] For provisions that have no subindex values listed, jurisdiction is given a subindex value of 10 if its law is in full compliance with the recommendation, or 0 otherwise.

the notice required, the higher the standard. The jurisdiction is given a 10 if the provision requires the employer to notify the employees directly rather than merely notifying the union or the government. Finally, a provision that requires at least some severance pay is assigned a weight of 0.20, on the grounds that jurisdictions that grant employees monetary compensation associated with the loss of a job have a higher standard than jurisdictions that do not require the employer to pay monetary compensation.

A requirement that the union be notified is weighted at 0.10. The standard is presumed to be higher if the employees can obtain aid from a union. Moreover, notification to the union would facilitate the filing of any grievances under the collective agreement. This provision is assigned a weight that is half of those of the major provisions because union coverage is far less than 100 percent.

The maximum time in which the layoffs must occur, once notification has been given, is assigned a score of 0.04, since it involves a question of when the employees know with certainty that their positions will end. It is presumed that the shorter the time, the higher the standard, as a shorter period results in increased certainty. Additionally, a long delay in layoff can result in a dilution of the purpose of the notice provision, because employees are unable to allocate full time to a job search.

In addition to appeal rights, the other provision with a positive weight is notice to the government. If such notice is required, the government can more easily notify laid-off employees of government services, and also investigate the employer if there have been any violations of the law.

SUMMARY

This chapter explains the weights and subindex values created for each of the 10 labor standards analyzed. Although there may be legitimate differences of opinion regarding individual weights and subindices, we believe that the ones we use are logical, defensible, and, where appropriate, grounded in the academic literature.[26] Moreover, because

we will provide the composition of each of the indices, other researchers can easily recompute the indices to suit their own needs.

Notes

1. For a discussion of the Canadian constitutional basis of this system, see Car-
    rothers 1986.
2. The labor standards in the following sectors are federally regulated in Canada: air
    transportation, banking, broadcasting, communications, Crown corporations
    (such as Canada Post), flour, feed mills, grain elevators, longshoring, interprovin-
    cial and international railways, interprovincial and international road transport,
    shipping and navigation, and various miscellaneous industries.   See Canada
    Labour Relations Board 1991; Block 1997b.
3. The full spreadsheets showing each statutory provision within each jurisdiction
    are available upon request.
4. Our initial intention in this portion of the research was to focus on two aspects of
    enforcement: 1) the aggressiveness of enforcement efforts by the jurisdiction, and
    2) the rights of appeal by litigants. It seemed reasonable to measure the aggres-
    siveness of an agency by calculating its budget deflated by a measure of employee
    coverage, on the presumption that greater resources in an agency would indicate
    greater enforcement powers. The assumption implicit in this view, however, was
    that agencies enforcing comparable standards across jurisdictions performed com-
    parable functions. If that is not the case, then budgets cannot be compared. Once
    we began to analyze the differing systems of labor standards administration, not
    only between the two countries but also between jurisdictions within the two
    countries, it became clear that agencies are not comparable. For example, the
    enforcement of equal opportunity laws in the United States is housed, in the first
    instance, in the Equal Employment Opportunity Commission (EEOC). The
    EEOC's jurisdiction is limited to matters of employment discrimination. More-
    over, it may only investigate complaints, attempt to conciliate, and sue in court. It
    is not a decision-making body. (See Title VII of the *Civil Rights Act of 1964*, Sec.
    705.)

    In Canada, however, the enforcement of employment equity laws is mainly
    housed in provincial human rights commissions, which generally have jurisdic-
    tion over all matters involving human rights, such as housing and public accom-
    modations as well as employment. Moreover, the commissions also make
    administrative decisions regarding violations of the provincial human rights stat-
    utes. (See, for example, Alberta Community Development, Alberta Human
    Rights, Citizenship and Multiculturalism Act [<http://www.gov.ab.ca/~mcd/citi-
    zen/hr/hrcmcact.htm>] and Alberta, "Quick Facts about the Human Rights, Citi-
    zenship and Multiculturalism Act" [<http://www.gov.ab.ca/~mcd/citizen/hr/pubs/
    quickfct/quickfct.htm>]; and Ontario, *Ontario Human Rights Code* [<http://
    www.ohrc.on.ca/english/codeeng.htm>].)

Similarly, the U.S. National Labor Relations Board has both adjudicative and prosecutorial functions (the latter through the Office of the General Counsel), and it must incorporate both in its budget. Canadian boards have no such prosecutorial function, and thus no need to budget for it. See, for example, Bruce 1990 and Block 1994.

5. The term "agency," in this context, refers to a duly empowered, individual decision maker in the agency, or a tribunal, board, or commission operating within the agency. The key question is the extent to which the internal decision of the agency, whatever the procedure by which it was reached, can be appealed externally to a court.

6. Paragraph 86, Sec. 3, at <http://149.174.222.20/WCB/WCB.nsf/Public/WCACTsect86>.

7. 29 U.S.C. 160(f).

8. For similar language on judicial review of decisions of the Occupational Safety and Health Review Commission, created under the *United States Occupational Safety and Health Act*, see 29 U.S.C. 660(a), at <http://www.law.cornell.edu:80/uscode/29/660.html>.

9. 340 U.S. 474, 1951.

10. Block and Wolkinson (1985) argued that the courts are unwilling to defer to the NLRB because the NLRB is limited to interpreting the National Labor Relations Act, while the courts have the authority to attempt to harmonize the act's principles with other legal principles. They also contended that, whereas U.S. law views property rights as fundamental constitutional rights, worker rights are statutory-based. Thus, when employers exercise property rights, they are exercising a higher order of rights.

   Brudney (1996) pointed out that the courts of appeal give far more weight to employee free choice than to employer deterrence and bargaining stability; the latter two values are important to the NLRB. This is part of what Brudney calls "statutory aging"—a process by which the courts are attempting to harmonize a mid 1930s statute (which was designed to encourage collectivization of the employment relationship, to encourage industrial stability, and to increase mass purchasing power) with contemporary values such as employee freedom of choice and the protection of individual rights at the workplace.

11. We do not include appeals rights or judicial review as a consideration in unemployment insurance (United States) or employment insurance (Canada). Although there may be a dispute over whether any individual employee qualifies for insurance, such cases are highly individual and have no effect on the general standards.

12. We include an additional element in the workers' compensation enforcement measures: the scope of appeal within the workers' compensation adjudicative system. Typically, jurisdictions allow either a narrow review based solely on a point of law or a more complete one that permits a full review of the record, sometimes to the point of a *de novo* appeal. The index used here gives a jurisdiction a score of 0 if the appeal process permits a review beyond solely the basis of law, on the

assumption that the fuller the review of the record (and possibly the evidence), the longer the process is likely to be. Although the Canadian provinces typically do not allow appeals outside the administrative system, an appeal within the system can be brought on a basis wider than a mere point of law.

13. For a somewhat comparable process of coding legislation, albeit only for public sector collective bargaining laws, see Currie and McConnell (1991) and Gunderson, Hebdon, and Hyatt (1996).

14. We are aware that, to some extent, the indices are a function of the weights given to each relevant provision. Although the weights are open to debate, we believe that the weighting scheme we have developed is reasonable. Other weighting schemes are likely equally reasonable. See the Chapter 5 appendix for a test of the robustness of the weights.

15. There are no occupational or industrial exclusions from judicially determined exceptions to employment-at-will in the United States.

16. The only departure from this assumption is for British Columbia, where managers are exempt.

17. Total employment for Yukon and the Northwest Territories was not included in the data set. The employment totals for these two jurisdictions were taken from the following Internet addresses: <http://www.yukonweb.com/government/facts.htmld /#earnings> and <http://www.stats.gov.nt.ca/Bureau/StatInfo/LabourForce/_LfsData.html>.

18. See, for example, *NLRB v. Bell Aerospace*, 416 U.S. 267 (1974); *Health Care and Retirement Systems v. NLRB*, 511 U.S. 571 (1994); and *NLRB v. Kentucky River Community Care Inc.*, U.S. Supreme Court, No. 99-1815 (2001) at <http://www.findlaw.com/casecode/supreme.html>, party name search = "Kentucky River."

19. Among others listed, the following sources were used to obtain or compute the provisions in the indices: Bureau of National Affairs (1994, 1995a,b,c); Government of Canada (1988, 1993, 1995); Canada Labour Relations Board (1991); Commerce Clearinghouse Inc. (various years); Hardin et al. (1990 and updates); Human Resources Development Canada (1995a,b,c, 1997, 1998a,b); Kumar (1991); and U.S. Department of Labor (1998).

20. We do not consider the question of whether payroll taxes are truly borne by the employer or are fully or partly shifted to employees in the form of reduced compensation. We note that it is also possible that, when employees have market power, they can conceivably shift part of their tax back to the employer by demanding higher compensation. Because there is no way of knowing which effect operates, we simply assume that the total cost of the tax is borne by the party that directly pays the tax.

21. See Ballantyne and Mazingo (1999) for data used to code levels of appeal.

22. We presume that union organizing rights and employee rights coincide, and that standards that favor union organizing also favor employees. This is because, in collective bargaining, unions are the institutional actor that represents employees. Although it may be argued that enhancing the rights of unions does not necessar-

ily enhance the rights of employees, especially the rights of those employees who may oppose union representation, it would be methodologically impossible to determine the percentage of employees who might feel a loss of welfare if union rights were enhanced.   Moreover, if there were an overvaluation of the enhancement of employee welfare based on the enhancement of union bargaining rights, that overvaluation would be limited to this component because the other components either address employee rights broadly or are generally operative when union representation has been selected.

23. See *Meritor Savings Bank v. Vinson*, 477 U.S. 57 (1986).

24. For example, the U.S. Supreme Court has ruled that for "hostile environment" sexual harassment to be shown, the actions in the workplace to which the employee objects must be severe and pervasive (*Harris v. Forklift Systems*, 63 FEP Cases, 225, 1993). It would be impossible to attempt to code the full range of actions that would be classified as "severe and pervasive," given the subjectivity of this standard. See, for example, *Faragher v. City of Boca Raton*, 97-282 (1998), in which the District Court and Supreme Court, on the one hand, and the Court of Appeals on the other, disagreed on whether the same set of facts constituted unlawful sexual harassment.

25. For a contrary view, see Krueger (1991).

26. For a similar colloquy, see Gunderson, Hebdon, and Hyatt (1996) and Currie and McConnell (1996).

5

The Results

U.S. and Canadian
Labor Standards Compared

OVERVIEW

The labor standards indices for the United States and Canada are summarized in Tables 5.1 and 5.2, respectively.[1] The second-to-last column in each shows the sums of the basic indices for each jurisdiction. The last column shows the sum of the coverage-deflated indices (the actual coverage-deflated indices are not included). The sums presented indicate the overall level of labor standards in each jurisdiction as of December 31, 1998.

Table 5.3 compares the indices for the two countries. The first two rows of Table 5.3 show the averages of the unweighted basic indices for the two countries as derived in Tables 5.1 and 5.2, and then a sum of the unweighted averages. The last two rows of Table 5.3 present the indices weighting the jurisdictions by the percentage of the country's employment[2] in each jurisdiction. Although the differences between the unweighted and employment-weighted indices are not great, some are noticeable. Table 5.4 presents analogous information for the coverage-deflated indices.

Comparing the range of U.S. indices (Table 5.1) with those in Canada (Table 5.2) we see that, in general, Canadian labor standards are higher than U.S. labor standards, as measured by the procedure outlined in Chapter 4. The U.S. basic indices range from 47.58 (Tennessee) to 61.77 (Montana), while the Canadian basic indices range from 54.79 (Alberta) to 76.10 (British Columbia). The U.S. coverage-deflated indices range from 43.83 (Tennessee) to 60.66 (Montana) compared with a Canadian range of 51.56 (Alberta) to 72.38 (British Columbia).

That Canadian labor standards are higher than U.S. labor standards is corroborated in Tables 5.3 and 5.4, which present the results for averages for the basic labor standards indices and the coverage deflated labor standards indices, as measured by the procedure outlined in Chapter 4. As Table 5.3 shows, the sums of the basic unweighted indices for the United States and Canada are 52.24 and 64.28, respectively. The sums of the employment-weighted basic indices for the United States and Canada (weighted by provincial or state employment) are 51.91 and 65.27, respectively. Table 5.4, presenting coverage-deflated indices, shows results comparable to those for the basic indices. The sums of the unweighted indices are 49.92 and 63.10 for the United States and Canada, respectively. The sums of the employment-weighted indices are 50.23 and 64.20, respectively, for the United States and Canada.[3]

STATISTICAL RESULTS: NONPARAMETRIC ANALYSIS

The above discussion is based solely on a descriptive comparison and does not provide a statistical test of the differences in the labor standards. The differences in these indices cannot be subject to testing with standard parametric statistical techniques. Although it is helpful to use averages to illustrate the points, we assume that the indices do not have any distribution, normal or otherwise; thus they should be analyzed using nonparametric techniques. Therefore, we base our statistical comparison of the labor standards in the two countries on the ranking of each of the jurisdictions for each of the standards.

In this procedure, we rank each of the 63 (51 in the United States and 12 in Canada) political jurisdictions according to its subindex value on the basic, unweighted indices on each of the standards. For each standard, the jurisdiction with the highest index on that standard is ranked 1 for that standard, and the jurisdiction with the lowest index on that standard is ranked 63. An adjusted ranking is created by assigning jurisdictions with equal scores a rank equal to the mean of the ranks associated with that index value. For example, if two jurisdictions have the highest possible score on a standard, each is assigned a rank of

1.5—that is, $(1 + 2)/2$. With this method, lower index values are associated with better ranks and thus higher labor standards.

The ranks for each of the 10 standards for each jurisdiction are then summed.[4] Therefore, the best possible score (the highest labor standard) for a jurisdiction is 10 (that is, 10 standards each ranked first; 10 $\times$ 1). The worst possible score for a jurisdiction is 630 (10 standards, each ranked 63rd; 10 $\times$ 63).

Table 5.5 presents the raw results of these rankings. As can be seen, 6 of the 10 jurisdictions with the best rankings are Canadian, including two of the three largest provinces: Ontario and British Columbia. Nine of the 12 Canadian provinces or territories are in the upper half of the distribution.

Despite what appear to be consistently higher labor standards there, the provincial autonomy in Canada, in contrast to U.S. federal supremacy, results in a greater range of sums of adjusted rankings in Canada than in the United States. Thus, in Canada, the range of the sums of adjusted ranks is 268 (the sum in British Columbia is 108.5; whereas it is 376.5 in Alberta), while the range of the sums of adjusted ranks in the United States is 181.5 (Hawaii is 217.5; whereas Delaware is 399.5).

To determine if the differences between the United States and Canada are significant, we tested Mann-Whitney and Wilcoxon rank difference tests for comparing populations. We tested the rankings on each of the standards and the sums of each of the standards to determine if these differences could have occurred by chance (Mendenhall, Schaeffer, and Wackerly 1986). These tests do not require that the samples be of equal size, and they assume no underlying distribution. The null hypothesis is that the jurisdiction rankings for the two countries are drawn from populations with identical distributions—that is, there is no significant difference in the ranks of the jurisdictions by country.

The results, presented in Table 5.6, show that the Canadian ranks are significantly better than the U.S. ranks on 6 of the 10 standards: paid time off, unemployment or employment insurance (UI/EI), workers' compensation, collective bargaining, unjust discharge, and advance notice of large-scale layoffs. The U.S. ranks are significantly better than the Canadian ranks on three standards: minimum wage, overtime, and occupational safety and health. There is no significant difference between the two countries in the rankings on the equal employment opportunity or employment equity (EEO/EE) standard.

RESULTS ON INDIVIDUAL LABOR STANDARDS

This section discusses the results for each standard, focusing first on standards that require employer payments, and then turning to standards that place constraints on employer actions vis-à-vis employees.

Minimum Wage

Table 5.7 presents the scoring of the components used to construct the minimum wage index. Although minimum wage levels, denominated in domestic dollars, were generally higher in Canada as of December 31, 1998, than in the United States,[5] in order to make comparisons between the two countries, the minimum wage rates were evaluated in U.S.$. To smooth fluctuations in the exchange rate, an average over the 1994–1998 period was used, where Can$1 = U.S.$.71 (or U.S.$1 = Can$.40).[6] Evaluated in a common currency, the U.S. minimum wage rates were higher than those in Canada. The Canadian minimum wage, valued in U.S. dollars, ranged from $4.22 to $5.08. The combined effects of recent increases in the U.S. statutory minimum wage rate and an exchange rate in which the Canadian dollar has been devalued relative to the U.S. dollar places the U.S. rates above all of the Canadian jurisdictions for this standard. This current difference is reflected in country-level minimum wage indices that average 7.24 for the United States, 4.07 for Canada for the unweighted minimum wage index, and 7.34 and 5.24 for the employment-weighted index, as shown in Table 5.3. The reason for the greater difference in the employment-weighted and unweighted minimum wage indices in Canada relative to the United States is because of the relatively high minimum wage rates in the three largest provinces, Ontario, Quebec, and British Columbia. Recall that the unweighted index weights all provinces and territories equally, while the employment-weighted index gives greater weight in computing the index to the larger provinces.

Overtime and Hours of Work

Table 5.8 presents the jurisdiction indices for the overtime standard. Basic overtime standards are higher in the United States than in Canada for several reasons. First, the federal standard in the United States is a maximum of 40 hours accumulated in a single work week. There is far more variation in this norm in Canada. Of the 13 Canadian labor standards jurisdictions, only 7 have a 40-hour per week maximum. New Brunswick and Ontario use 44 hours; Quebec has a 43-hour standard; and Nova Scotia and Prince Edward Island have enacted a 48-hour straight-time maximum. Second, in three Canadian provinces (New Brunswick, Nova Scotia, and Newfoundland), the overtime rate is a multiple of the minimum wage rate rather than the individual's straight-time rate.

Both countries permit sectoral exemptions, generally for those industries that either do not operate on a regular daily work schedule or whose employees must perform their jobs without supervision and monitoring. Quebec is the only jurisdiction in either country that permits an exception either by collective agreement or with the permission of the government.

The index averages (shown in Table 5.3) reflect this difference: for the unweighted basic indices, the average is 10 for the United States and 7.49 for Canada; for the employment-weighted indices, the averages are 10 for the United States and 7.06 for Canada. When coverage is taken into account, the differences narrow: the unweighted for the United States average is 8.68, and for Canada, 6.47; the comparable employment-weighted figures are 8.83 and 6.41.[7]

Paid Time Off

Table 5.9 presents the results for paid time off in the United States and Canada. Although most states have more official holidays than Canadian jurisdictions do, there is no requirement in any law or statute in the United States that employees be paid for those holidays. But mandatory payment to employees for official holidays is almost universal throughout Canada. Every Canadian jurisdiction requires that employees either be paid time and a half, if they must work an official holiday, or receive the day off with pay.

In addition to these differences, Canadian jurisdictions, unlike those in the United States, have legislatively mandated paid vacations. Mandated vacations range from two to three weeks, with employees receiving 4 percent or 6 percent of their annual pay. A person is eligible after being employed from 10 to 12 months, depending on the jurisdiction.

It is clear that Canadian standards for paid time off are far higher than comparable U.S. standards. The paid time off index reflects this difference. Because the greatest weight is assigned to the pay entitlement provision (which gets twice the weight given to the number of holidays in the jurisdiction), the Canadian indices are far higher than those in the United States. As shown in Table 5.3, the undeflated, unweighted indices are 1.29 and 6.37 for the United States and Canada, respectively. The comparable employment-weighted numbers are 1.29 and 6.59. Deflating for coverage makes only a small difference, as is evident in Table 5.4 The U.S. indices do not change, as there is no legislated paid time off in the United States, and holidays apply to all employees. Deflating for coverage reduces the Canadian indices to 6.31 and 6.02 for the unweighted and employment-weighted indices, respectively.

Unemployment or Employment Insurance

Table 5.10 presents the results for the unemployment insurance (UI) system in the United States and the employment insurance (EI) system in Canada. Our results and indices suggest that the Canadian EI system is slightly better, from the workers' point of view, than the U.S. UI systems. Although, as shown in Table 5.3, the difference between the two countries' unweighted averages is relatively small (6.28 compared with 7.51), 47 of the 51 U.S. jurisdictions (50 states and the District of Columbia) have indices below the Canadian national index, suggesting that few U.S. workers are governed by a statute as generous as Canada's.

This difference in favor of Canada is due to two factors. First, the average weekly benefit as a percentage of previous earnings in Canada is higher than in the United States. The Canadian is 55 percent, while in the United States the average is 37 percent. Second, Canadian workers may draw their benefits for a longer time than U.S. workers—45 weeks as compared with a maximum of approximately 39 weeks (with extended benefits) in the United States. The typical length of time in the United States is 26 weeks.

While the benefit structure to employees is higher in Canada than in the United States, Canadian workers must pay for these higher benefits. In the United States (exception of Alaska), the total cost of UI is borne by employers, while in Canada the cost of EI is shared: Canadian employees pay $2.95 per $100 of insurable earnings up to earnings of $39,000 per year; U.S. workers pay nothing. This somewhat offsets the advantage that unemployed Canadian workers have vis-à-vis their counterparts in the United States.[8]

Workers' Compensation

Tables 5.11a, b, and c present the results for the workers' compensation indices for the United States and Canada. The criteria used to represent the program dimensions of workers' compensation are based on the 19 essential recommendations from the report of the National Commission on State Workmen's Compensation Laws (1972), with 8 related to coverage, 9 related to income benefit adequacy, and 2 to medical benefit adequacy.

As shown in Table 5.3, the average unweighted base indices for the two countries are 6.72 and 7.60 for the United States and Canada, respectively. Weighting changes these scores to 6.58 and 7.77, respectively. Fourteen jurisdictions (Connecticut, District of Columbia, Hawaii, Iowa, Illinois, Montana, New Hampshire, Ohio, Rhode Island, Utah, Washington, Wisconsin, and West Virginia) have indices greater than the Canadian unweighted, undeflated standard. Three Canadian provinces (Alberta, Manitoba, and New Brunswick) have indices lower than the U.S. unweighted, undeflated standard. The primary explanation for the higher Canadian indices are the appeal processes, somewhat higher death benefits, and an absence of limitation on the duration of temporary total benefits. Overall, these results indicate greater compliance with the essential recommendations in Canada than in the United States.

Looking at the subcomponents of the essential recommendations of the National Commission, the Canadian laws are more complete with respect to coverage and slightly less complete with respect to benefit levels. Although actual benefit levels tend to be slightly higher in Canada than in the United States, the Canadian provinces in general provide slightly less extensive benefits to widows and survivors in the event of death.

CONSTRAINING EMPLOYER ALLOCATION OF LABOR

Collective Bargaining

Table 5.12 presents the results for the collective bargaining indices for the United States and Canada. As is generally acknowledged, Canadian labor laws are far more favorable to unions and collective activity than U.S. labor laws. Of the seven scoring components for collective bargaining, the United States is scored zero for all but the statutory protection of bargaining collectively. Eleven of the 13 Canadian jurisdictions require no election for union certification, thus minimizing the role of the employer in the unionization process. None of the Canadian jurisdictions places limits on the scope of bargaining, thus permitting union involvement in a wide range of employer decisions. All Canadian jurisdictions have procedures under which either one party or the government may require conciliation during negotiations, thus making it more difficult than otherwise for the employer to use the bargaining process to eliminate the union. Two jurisdictions have a broad-based ban on striker replacements, and seven jurisdictions permit first-agreement arbitration, thus institutionalizing the union.

These differences result in a substantially higher index for the Canadian jurisdictions than for the United States. As shown in Table 5.3, the nondeflated, unweighted Canadian index is 7.92, as compared to an index of 1.50 for the United States. The weighted Canadian average is 7.10, while the U.S. average, because it is based on national legislation, does not change. The change in the Canadian index is due to the greater weight associated with Ontario, which has relatively weak collective bargaining legislation, relative to the other provinces. An examination of Table 5.4, showing coverage deflated indices, shows lower levels, but the basic conclusion of substantially higher indices for Canadian workers relative to U.S. workers does not change.

Equal Employment Opportunity/Employment Equity

Table 5.13 presents the results for the equal employment opportunity (United States) and employment equity (Canada) indices. The EEO/EI index, which is heavily weighted toward racial and gender discrimination protection, indicates that this labor standard in the two countries is roughly equal. As shown in Table 5.3, the relevant unweighted basic index averages are 8.64 in the United States and 8.68 in Canada. The weighted index averages are 8.76 in the United States and 8.53 in Canada. The slight drop for Canada is due to the fact that the largest province, Ontario, was associated with an index slightly lower than the unweighted average. The average of the coverage-deflated indices, shown in Table 5.4, are comparable to the nondeflated averages shown in Table 5.3.

The table indicates that Canadian law covers a slightly wider range of activities and classes than U.S. law. Laws in both countries cover race, Aboriginal peoples, and visible minorities; gender; national origin or ancestry; religion; and age. More Canadian provinces than U.S. states cover sexual orientation. In addition, most Canadian jurisdictions protect persons from discrimination based on political beliefs and membership in organizations, protection that is not extended to employees or applicants in the United States (with the exception of union membership). U.S. law, on the other hand, goes further than most Canadian jurisdictions in requiring reasonable accommodation for disabled employees (Schneid 1992).

A key difference, albeit uncoded, between EEO law in the United States, and EE law in Canada is that the latter is grounded in concepts of human rights comparable to constitutional rights in the United States, while the former is viewed as a regulation of interstate commerce. In the United States, there has been a reluctance to permit employees to make constitutional claims against private employers (Kelly 1991; Wolkinson and Block 1996).

Unjust Dismissal

Table 5.14 presents the results for the unjust discharge indices for the United States and Canada. With the exception of Montana, no jurisdiction in either country has broad-based protection against unjust dismissal. In the United States, roughly 40 states have developed judicial doctrine based on contract law that prohibits an employer from discharging an employee except for just cause if the employer has contracted not to do so. Such contracts may be written, implied, or based on a handbook. Other states have also created exceptions for employees who are discharged for refusing to violate public policy or who are discharged when an employer refuses to pay for benefits already earned (for example, sales commissions).

Canadian law has developed a broad-based notice requirement (Human Resources Development Canada 1995b; Levitt 1985). Thus, employers who terminate employees without giving proper notice will generally be required to pay the employee what he or she would have received during the notice period. The notice requirement increases with the length of time on the job.

It thus appears that Canadian employees have a greater level of protection against unjust discharge than U.S. employees. Protection in the United States is generally limited to those employees who can demonstrate an employer promise. Protection in Canada is based on employment status, per se. This difference is reflected in the coding of our index. We give the greatest weight to the coverage breadth of the Canadian statutes. Conversely, the situation-specific nature of unjust discharge protection in the United States caused us to give it a narrow weight. Thus, all the Canadian jurisdictions have an index value of 7, while the states generally have indices between 2 and 3.

Occupational Safety and Health

Tables 5.15a and b present the components of the occupational safety and health indices for the United States and Canada. Although it is impossible to analyze detailed regulations for each industry, a comparison of procedures and penalties suggests that U.S. federal safety and health standards are somewhat higher than the standards in most of the Canadian provinces. The U.S. index score is 3.13, as shown in Table 5.3, while the nondeflated, unweighted Canadian average is 2.78. This advantage to the United States is primarily due to the higher penalties the United States imposes. On the other hand, the data indicate that two of the three largest provinces, Ontario and British Columbia, have fairly high health and safety standards. The standards in Quebec, however, are low relative to the other provinces.

Advance Notice of Plant Closings and Large-Scale Layoffs

Table 5.16 presents the components of the advance notice indices for the United States and Canada. The components incorporated into this index include the minimum number of employees necessary to trigger a requirement, the amount of advance notice required, whether notice is given to the affected employees, whether there is a severance pay requirement, and whether notice must also be given to the union, if the employees are so represented. It should be noted that the severance pay requirements refer to individual as opposed to group termination. There are no statutory requirements in the United States that employees be paid severance pay. However, Canadian employees under federal jurisdiction or in British Columbia or Ontario are entitled to severance pay if they meet the qualifying tenure requirements. The United States has enacted national legislation, the Worker Adjustment and Retraining Notification Act (WARN). Canadian provinces determine the extent of advance notice for firms within their borders.

As shown in Table 5.3, the nondeflated, unweighted indices indicate that the United States has slightly better advance notice provisions than Canada. The nondeflated, unweighted indices are 5.03 for the United States and 4.87 for Canada, as shown in Table 5.4. The coverage-deflated weighted indices are 5.03 and 4.82, respectively.

These indices are somewhat misleading, however, since the Canadian scores are influenced by the provinces of Alberta and Prince Edward Island, neither of which has advance notice provisions. If we compute a Canadian index including only the provinces that have advance notice provisions, the nondeflated and coverage-deflated, unweighted averages for Canada increase to 5.76 and 5.78, respectively,[9] showing that the Canadian jurisdictions that have enacted advance notice provisions have stricter provisions than WARN in the United States.

SUMMARY AND CONCLUSIONS

The results presented in this chapter indicate that, overall, labor standards are higher in Canada than in the United States. These conclusions are suggested by the total of the index scores for each of the standards and for each of the jurisdictions. The results are confirmed by the analysis of the rankings of each of the 63 jurisdictions on the labor standards.

Despite the significance of this generalization, the results on the individual standards are also important, because not all labor standards will be equally important in all industries. The rankings analysis suggests that labor standards are higher in Canada than in the United States on three of the five standards requiring employer payments— paid time off, UI/EI, and workers' compensation. Overtime requirements are actually more stringent in the United States than in Canada. Moreover, to the extent that U.S. employers provide vacation and holiday pay to their employees, the gap between the two countries would be narrowed further. Overall, then, although direct payments associated with employment are greater for Canadian employers than for their United States counterparts, the difference may be small.

Turning to the standards constraining employer allocation of labor, it is clear that Canadian standards are substantially higher than U.S. standards for collective bargaining and unjust discharge, and slightly higher for advance notice, where such requirements exist in Canada. Antidiscrimination laws are comparable in both countries, and the United States may actually provide greater penalties for violation of health and safety laws than does Canada. Although Canada does have slightly more stringent requirements than the United States for notification regarding plant closing and large scale layoffs, there is a question regarding the frequency with which the obligations under such a statute would be triggered for any employers. On the other hand, standards for collective bargaining, unjust dismissal restrictions, and occupational safety and health operate daily at the workplace.

The foregoing discussion suggests the importance of decomposing the standards. We discuss this matter further in Chapter 6.

Table 5.1 Basic and Coverage-Deflated Labor Standards Indices, United States, as of December 31, 1998

| | Standards requiring employer payments | | | | | Standards constraining employer allocation of labor | | | | | | |
Jurisdiction	Minimum wage	Overtime	Paid time off	UI/EI	Workers' compensation	Collective bargaining	EEO/EE	Unjust discharge	Occupational safety and health	Advance notice	Sum of basic indices[a]	Sum of coverage-deflated index[b]
AL	6.84	10.00	1.29	5.12	5.67	1.50	8.35	3.00	3.13	5.03	49.92	46.01
AK	9.08	10.00	1.11	5.01	6.64	1.50	8.35	3.00	3.13	5.03	52.83	51.28
AZ	6.84	10.00	1.11	5.58	6.02	1.50	8.35	3.00	3.13	5.03	50.55	46.52
AR	6.84	10.00	1.11	6.77	5.26	1.50	8.35	2.00	3.13	5.03	49.98	49.14
CA	9.60	10.00	1.11	5.02	6.92	1.50	9.35	3.00	3.13	5.03	54.64	53.22
CO	6.84	10.00	1.11	6.33	7.07	1.50	8.85	3.00	3.13	5.03	52.85	50.93
CT	9.08	10.00	1.11	5.74	7.94	1.50	9.35	3.00	3.13	5.03	55.87	54.18
DE	6.84	10.00	1.47	5.58	5.69	1.50	8.35	1.50	3.13	5.03	49.08	45.13
DC	10.00	10.00	1.29	5.74	8.65	1.50	8.85	2.50	3.13	5.03	56.68	54.92
FL	6.84	10.00	1.11	6.17	5.77	1.50	8.85	1.00	3.13	5.03	49.39	48.11
GA	6.84	10.00	1.65	5.58	5.34	1.50	8.35	1.00	3.13	5.03	48.41	46.58
HI	7.76	10.00	1.29	8.58	7.91	1.50	9.35	2.50	3.13	5.03	57.04	55.60
ID	6.84	10.00	1.29	7.27	5.13	1.50	8.35	3.00	3.13	5.03	51.52	48.85
IL	7.24	10.00	1.29	6.17	7.86	1.50	8.35	2.00	3.13	5.03	52.56	50.82
IN	6.84	10.00	1.65	5.58	6.13	1.50	8.35	1.50	3.13	5.03	49.70	45.81
IA	6.84	10.00	1.29	7.10	8.10	1.50	8.35	2.75	3.13	5.03	54.07	49.90
KS	6.84	10.00	1.29	6.77	6.52	1.50	8.85	2.00	3.13	5.03	51.92	50.14
KY	6.84	10.00	1.47	6.17	7.55	1.50	8.85	2.25	3.13	5.03	52.78	51.34

(continued)

Table 5.1 (continued)

Juris-diction	Standards requiring employer payments					Standards constraining employer allocation of labor					Sum of basic indices[a]	Sum of coverage-deflated index[b]
	Minimum wage	Overtime	Paid time off	UI/EI	Workers' com-pensation	Collective bar-gaining	EEO/EE	Unjust dis-charge	Occupa-tional safety and health	Advance notice		
LA	6.84	10.00	1.65	5.02	5.38	1.50	8.85	1.25	3.13	5.03	48.64	44.75
ME	6.84	10.00	1.29	6.17	7.31	1.50	8.85	1.50	3.13	5.03	51.62	49.27
MD	7.24	10.00	1.47	5.58	7.27	1.50	9.35	2.00	3.13	5.03	52.56	50.38
MA	7.76	10.00	1.29	7.55	7.31	1.50	8.35	2.75	3.13	5.03	54.66	53.08
MI	6.84	10.00	1.47	6.17	5.81	1.50	8.85	2.50	3.13	5.03	51.30	50.65
MN	6.84	10.00	1.29	7.10	7.20	1.50	8.85	2.00	3.13	5.03	52.93	50.93
MS	6.84	10.00	1.29	5.58	4.76	1.50	8.35	2.25	3.13	5.03	48.72	45.34
MO	6.84	10.00	1.29	5.58	7.78	1.50	8.85	3.00	3.13	5.03	52.99	51.31
MT	7.24	10.00	1.11	7.10	7.83	1.50	8.85	10.00	3.13	5.03	61.77	60.66
NE	7.24	10.00	1.47	5.58	7.15	1.50	8.35	2.25	3.13	5.03	51.69	47.49
NV	7.04	10.00	1.29	6.50	6.37	1.50	8.35	2.75	3.13	5.03	51.95	50.14
NH	6.84	10.00	1.47	5.58	8.85	1.50	8.35	3.00	3.13	5.03	53.74	52.75
NJ	7.24	10.00	1.47	6.50	4.61	1.50	8.35	2.00	3.13	5.03	49.82	49.19
NM	6.84	10.00	1.29	5.74	4.70	1.50	8.85	2.50	3.13	5.03	49.57	47.91
NY	6.84	10.00	1.29	5.58	5.89	1.50	8.85	1.00	3.13	5.03	49.10	48.55
NC	6.84	10.00	1.47	6.33	7.47	1.50	8.35	2.00	3.13	5.03	52.11	50.13
ND	6.84	10.00	1.11	6.93	6.95	1.50	9.35	1.75	3.13	5.03	52.58	49.67
OH	6.84	10.00	1.11	6.17	8.33	1.50	8.85	2.50	3.13	5.03	53.45	51.03
OK	6.84	10.00	1.11	6.93	5.89	1.50	8.35	2.00	3.13	5.03	50.77	46.71

OR	9.60	10.00	0.92	6.67	7.70	1.50	8.35	2.50	3.13	5.03	55.40	53.52
PA	6.84	10.00	1.29	6.76	7.31	1.50	8.85	1.75	3.13	5.03	52.45	51.01
RI	6.84	10.00	1.47	7.66	7.83	1.50	8.85	1.75	3.13	5.03	54.05	52.77
SC	6.84	10.00	1.11	6.17	6.13	1.50	8.35	2.50	3.13	5.03	50.75	46.90
SD	6.84	10.00	1.29	6.17	7.55	1.50	8.35	2.00	3.13	5.03	51.85	50.73
TN	6.84	10.00	1.65	5.58	3.51	1.50	8.35	2.00	3.13	5.03	47.58	43.83
TX	6.84	10.00	1.29	6.17	5.26	1.50	8.35	2.50	3.13	5.03	50.07	46.09
UT	6.84	10.00	1.29	7.10	7.86	1.50	8.35	2.50	3.13	5.03	53.59	49.70
VT	7.76	10.00	1.11	6.17	7.27	1.50	8.85	2.50	3.13	5.03	53.31	51.36
VA	6.84	10.00	1.29	6.17	6.26	1.50	8.85	2.25	3.13	5.03	51.31	47.12
WA	9.08	10.00	1.29	7.89	7.78	1.50	8.85	2.00	3.13	5.03	56.54	54.50
WV	6.84	10.00	1.47	6.17	8.38	1.50	8.35	2.50	3.13	5.03	53.36	52.22
WI	6.84	10.00	1.47	6.93	7.86	1.50	8.85	2.00	3.13	5.03	53.60	51.24
WY	6.84	10.00	0.92	6.93	4.83	1.50	8.35	3.00	3.13	5.03	50.52	46.31

a Sum may not equal total of subindices due to rounding.
b Coverage-deflated subindices themselves are not shown.

Table 5.2 Basic Indices and Sum of Coverage-Deflated Labor Standards Indices, Canada, December 31, 1998

Juris-diction	Standards requiring employer payments					Standards constraining employer allocation of labor					Sum of basic indices[a]	Sum of coverage-deflated index[b]
	Minimum wage	Overtime	Paid time off	UI/EI	Workers' com-pensation	Collective bar-gaining	EEO\EE	Unjust discharge	Occupa-tional safety and health	Advance notice		
Federal	4.28	10.00	6.27	7.51	6.77	6.00	9.00	7.00	4.33	5.53	66.69	[c]
AB	1.52	7.28	7.61	7.51	6.69	6.00	8.10	7.00	3.07	0.00	54.79	51.56
BC	7.04	10.00	6.27	7.51	8.58	10.00	8.60	7.00	3.20	7.89	76.10	72.38
MB	2.44	10.00	5.89	7.51	6.54	9.00	9.10	7.00	3.13	6.03	66.64	62.05
NB	2.44	3.21	5.38	7.51	5.99	8.00	8.10	7.00	2.11	5.71	55.44	53.11
NF	2.44	4.57	5.53	7.51	7.25	9.00	8.60	7.00	2.08	5.03	59.00	55.98
NT	6.12	10.00	6.27	7.51	8.82	6.00	9.00	7.00	2.18	3.21	66.11	63.18
NS	2.44	1.85	5.71	7.51	7.32	6.00	9.10	7.00	2.18	6.37	55.49	52.94
ON	6.12	7.28	6.07	7.51	7.64	9.00	8.50	7.00	3.24	7.03	69.39	65.48
PE	2.44	5.92	5.20	7.51	7.72	9.00	8.60	7.00	1.87	0.00	55.25	52.12
QC	6.12	7.28	7.23	7.51	8.35	10.00	9.00	7.00	2.63	4.50	69.62	66.38
SK	2.44	10.00	9.11	7.51	8.66	9.00	8.60	7.00	3.00	6.87	72.19	68.04
YT	7.04	10.00	6.27	7.51	8.43	6.00	8.50	7.00	3.17	5.21	69.13	66.18

[a] Sum may not equal total of subindices due to rounding.
[b] The coverage-deflated indices themselves are not shown.
[c] Not calculated because coverage is calculated by province.

Table 5.3 Employment-Weighted and Unweighted Average Basic Labor Standards Indices, United States and Canada, December 31, 1998

Juris-diction	Standards requiring employer payments					Standards constraining employer allocation of labor					Sum of basic indices[a]
	Minimum wage	Overtime	Paid time off	UI/EI	Workers' com-pensation	Collective bar-gaining	EEO\EE	Unjust discharge	Occupa-tional safety and health	Advance notice	
Unweighted average											
United States	7.24	10.00	1.29	6.28	6.72	1.50	8.64	2.41	3.13	5.03	52.24
Canada	4.07	7.49	6.37	7.51	7.60	7.92	8.68	7.00	2.78	4.87	64.30
Weighted average											
United States	7.34	10.00	1.29	6.09	6.58	1.50	8.76	2.19	3.13	5.03	51.91
Canada	5.24	7.06	6.59	7.51	7.77	7.10	8.53	7.00	2.81	5.66	65.27

[a] Sum may not equal total of subindices due to rounding.

Table 5.4 Employment-Weighted and Unweighted Average, Coverage-Deflated Labor Standards Indices, United States and Canada, December 31, 1998

| | Standards requiring employer payments | | | | | Standards constraining employer allocation of labor | | | | | |
Jurisdiction	Coverage-deflated minimum wage	Coverage-deflated overtime	Coverage-deflated paid-time off	Coverage-deflated UI/EI	Coverage-deflated workers' compensation	Coverage-deflated collective bargaining	Coverage-deflated EEO/EE	Coverage-deflated unjust discharge	Coverage-deflated occupational safety and health	Coverage-deflated advance notice	Sum[a]
Unweighted average											
United States	6.73	8.71	1.29	6.28	6.57	1.13	8.64	2.41	3.13	5.03	49.92
Canada	4.05	6.46	6.31	7.51	7.56	5.77	8.65	7.00	2.66	4.82	60.78
Weighted average											
United States	7.34	8.82	1.29	6.09	6.45	1.13	8.76	2.19	3.13	5.03	50.23
Canada	5.24	6.59	6.02	7.51	7.73	6.44	8.53	7.00	2.81	5.66	63.53

[a] Sum may not equal total of subindices due to rounding.

Table 5.5 Rankings for Canadian and U.S. Jurisdictions on Basic Unweighted Labor Standards Indices, December 31, 1998

Juris-diction	Standards requiring employee payments					Standards constraining employer allocation of labor					Overall ranking (sum of ranks)	Jurisdiction rank
	Minimum wage	Overtime	Paid time off	UI/EI	Workers' compensation	Collective bargaining	EEO/EE	Unjust discharge	Occupational safety and health	Advance notice		
BC	16.0	28.5	5.0	10.5	5.0	1.5	31.5	7.5	2.0	1.0	108.5	1.0
YT	16.0	28.5	5.0	10.5	8.0	10.5	34.5	7.5	3.0	7.0	130.5	2.0
ON	55.0	58.0	7.5	10.5	22.0	5.0	34.5	7.5	1.0	2.0	203.0	3.0
MB	59.5	28.5	7.5	10.5	47.0	5.0	6.5	7.5	29.5	5.0	206.5	4.0
SK	59.5	28.5	1.0	10.5	4.0	5.0	31.5	7.5	57.0	3.0	207.5	5.0
HI	8.0	28.5	38.0	1.0	6.0	38.0	3.0	32.0	29.5	33.5	217.5	6.0
MA	8.0	28.5	38.0	4.0	14.5	38.0	19.5	25.0	29.5	33.5	238.5	7.0
NT	55.0	28.5	5.0	10.5	2.0	10.5	8.5	7.5	59.5	61.0	248.0	8.0
MT	12.0	28.5	55.0	19.5	29.5	38.0	19.5	1.0	29.5	33.5	266.0	9.0
WA	5.0	28.5	38.0	2.0	26.5	38.0	19.5	47.5	29.5	33.5	268.0	10.0
NS	59.5	63.0	9.0	10.5	42.0	10.5	6.5	7.5	59.5	4.0	272.0	11.0
DC	1.0	28.5	38.0	47.0	9.0	38.0	19.5	32.0	29.5	33.5	276.0	12.0
CT	5.0	28.5	55.0	47.0	20.0	38.0	3.0	18.5	29.5	33.5	278.0	13.0
QC	55.0	60.0	3.0	10.5	10.0	1.5	8.5	7.5	63.0	60.0	279.0	14.0
MD	12.0	28.5	22.0	54.0	18.5	38.0	3.0	47.5	29.5	33.5	286.5	15.0
CA	2.5	28.5	55.0	61.5	21.0	38.0	3.0	18.5	29.5	33.5	291.0	16.0
RI	35.5	28.5	22.0	3.0	29.5	38.0	19.5	55.0	29.5	33.5	294.0	17.0
KY	35.5	28.5	22.0	39.5	11.0	38.0	19.5	39.5	29.5	33.5	296.5	18.0
IA	35.5	28.5	38.0	19.5	1.0	38.0	48.5	25.0	29.5	33.5	297.0	19.0

(continued)

Table 5.5 (continued)

Juris-diction	Standards requiring employee payments					Standards constraining employer allocation of labor					Overall ranking (sum of ranks)	Jurisdiction rank
	Minimum wage	Overtime	Paid time off	UI/EI	Workers' compensation	Collective bargaining	EEO/EE	Unjust discharge	Occupational safety and health	Advance notice		
WI	35.5	28.5	22.0	23.5	24.0	38.0	19.5	47.5	29.5	33.5	301.5	20.0
VT	8.0	28.5	55.0	39.5	18.5	38.0	19.5	32.0	29.5	33.5	302.0	21.0
NH	35.5	28.5	22.0	54.0	7.0	38.0	48.5	18.5	29.5	33.5	315.0	22.0
NF	*59.5*	*61.0*	*10.0*	*10.5*	*35.0*	*5.0*	*31.5*	*7.5*	*62.0*	*33.5*	*315.5*	*23.0*
PA	35.5	28.5	38.0	28.0	14.5	38.0	19.5	55.0	29.5	33.5	320.0	24.0
NJ	12.0	28.5	22.0	30.5	61.0	38.0	19.5	47.5	29.5	33.5	322.0	25.0
NE	12.0	28.5	22.0	54.0	17.0	38.0	48.5	39.5	29.5	33.5	322.5	26.0
WV	35.5	28.5	22.0	39.5	16.0	38.0	48.5	32.0	29.5	33.5	323.0	27.0
MI	35.5	28.5	22.0	39.5	46.0	38.0	19.5	32.0	29.5	33.5	324.0	28.0
OH	35.5	28.5	55.0	39.5	13.0	38.0	19.5	32.0	29.5	33.5	324.0	29.0
UT	35.5	28.5	38.0	19.5	24.0	38.0	48.5	32.0	29.5	33.5	327.0	30.0
NC	35.5	28.5	22.0	32.5	12.0	38.0	48.5	47.5	29.5	33.5	327.5	31.0
KS	35.5	28.5	38.0	26.5	33.5	38.0	19.5	47.5	29.5	33.5	330.0	32.0
MN	35.5	28.5	38.0	19.5	42.0	38.0	19.5	47.5	29.5	33.5	331.5	33.0
CO	35.5	28.5	55.0	32.5	42.0	38.0	19.5	18.5	29.5	33.5	332.5	34.0
OR	2.5	28.5	62.5	29.0	29.5	38.0	48.5	32.0	29.5	33.5	333.5	35.0
NB	*59.5*	*62.0*	*11.0*	*10.5*	*49.0*	*8.0*	*62.5*	*7.5*	*61.0*	*6.0*	*337.0*	*36.0*
ID	35.5	28.5	38.0	17.0	51.0	38.0	48.5	18.5	29.5	33.5	338.0	37.0
IL	12.0	28.5	38.0	39.5	24.0	38.0	48.5	47.5	29.5	33.5	339.0	38.0
PE	*59.5*	*58.0*	*12.0*	*10.5*	*36.0*	*5.0*	*31.5*	*7.5*	*58.0*	*62.5*	*340.5*	*39.0*
NV	35.5	28.5	38.0	30.5	38.0	38.0	48.5	25.0	29.5	33.5	345.0	40.0

VA	35.5	28.5	38.0	39.5	48.0	38.0	19.5	39.5	29.5	33.5	349.5	41.0
MO	35.5	28.5	38.0	54.0	26.5	38.0	48.5	18.5	29.5	33.5	350.5	42.0
ME	35.5	28.5	38.0	39.5	3.0	38.0	48.5	58.0	29.5	33.5	352.00	43.0
AK	5.0	28.5	55.0	63.0	37.0	38.0	48.5	18.5	29.5	33.5	356.5	44.0
NM	35.5	28.5	38.0	47.0	56.0	38.0	19.5	32.0	29.5	33.5	357.5	45.0
NY	16.0	28.5	38.0	54.0	57.5	38.0	3.0	62.0	29.5	33.5	360.0	46.0
SD	35.5	28.5	38.0	39.5	32.0	38.0	48.5	47.5	29.5	33.5	370.5	47.0
FL	35.5	28.5	55.0	39.5	33.5	38.0	19.5	62.0	29.5	33.5	374.5	48.0
AL	35.5	28.5	38.0	60.0	45.0	38.0	48.5	18.5	29.5	33.5	375.0	49.0
LA	35.5	28.5	14.5	61.5	55.0	38.0	19.5	60.0	29.5	33.5	375.5	50.0
AB	*63.0*	*58.0*	*2.0*	*10.5*	*44.0*	*10.5*	*62.5*	*7.5*	*56.0*	*62.5*	*376.5*	*51.0*
ND	35.5	28.5	55.0	23.5	29.5	38.0	48.5	55.0	29.5	33.5	376.5	52.0
WY	35.5	28.5	62.5	23.5	59.0	38.0	48.5	18.5	29.5	33.5	377.0	53.0
MS	35.5	28.5	38.0	54.0	62.5	38.0	19.5	39.5	29.5	33.5	378.5	54.0
IN	35.5	28.5	14.5	54.0	39.5	38.0	48.5	58.0	29.5	33.5	379.5	55.0
SC	35.5	28.5	55.0	39.5	39.5	38.0	48.5	32.0	29.5	33.5	379.5	56.0
TX	35.5	28.5	38.0	39.5	60.0	38.0	48.5	32.0	29.5	33.5	383.0	57.0
AZ	35.5	28.5	55.0	54.0	50.0	38.0	48.5	18.5	29.5	33.5	391.0	58.0
TN	35.5	28.5	14.5	54.0	62.5	38.0	48.5	47.5	29.5	33.5	392.0	59.0
AR	35.5	28.5	55.0	26.5	54.0	38.0	48.5	47.5	29.5	33.5	396.5	60.0
GA	35.5	28.5	14.5	54.0	53.0	38.0	48.5	62.0	29.5	33.5	397.0	61.0
OK	35.5	28.5	55.0	23.5	57.5	38.0	48.5	47.5	29.5	33.5	397.0	62.0
DE	35.5	28.5	22.0	54.0	52.0	38.0	48.5	58.0	29.5	33.5	399.5	63.0

NOTE: Canadian jurisdictions in italics.

Table 5.6 Results for Rank Difference Tests, U.S. and Canadian Basic Unweighted Labor Standards Indices, December 31, 1998

Jurisdiction	Standards requiring employer payments					Standards constraining employer allocation of labor					Mean
	Minimm wage	Overtime	Paid time off	UI/EI	Workers' compensation	Collective bargaining	EEO/EE	Unjust discharge	Occupational safety and health	Advance notice[c]	
Mean rank											
United States	27.43	28.50	38.00	37.06	34.65	38.00	32.67	37.76	29.50	33.50	36.02
Canada	51.42	46.88	6.50	10.50	20.75	6.50	29.17	7.50	42.50	25.63	14.92
Significance[a]	<0.00[b]	<0.00[b]	<0.00[c]	<0.00[c]	0.018[c]	<0.00[c]	0.530[d]	<0.00[c]	0.001[b]	0.043[c]	0.001[c]

[a] Mann-Whitney U/ and Wilcoxon Z tests.
[b] U.S. rankings significantly higher than Canadian rankings at 0.05 level.
[c] Canadian rankings significantly higher than U.S. rankings at 0.05 level.
[d] No significant difference.

Table 5.7 Component Scoring for Minimum Wage Index, United States and Canada, December 31, 1998

Juris-diction	Minimum wage provisions[a]				Index	Coverage	Coverage-deflated index
	Wage levels[b]	Inexper-ienced employees[c]	Fines or imprison-ment	Limits on appeal rights[d]			
UNITED STATES							
Federal	7	0	10	10	6.84	—[e]	—[e]
AL	7	0	10	10	6.84	0.93	6.33
AK	9	10	10	10	9.08	0.95	8.63
AZ	7	0	10	10	6.84	0.92	6.29
AR[f]	7	0	10	10	6.84	0.93	6.38
CA	10	0	10	10	9.60	0.96	9.20
CO	7	0	10	10	6.84	0.94	6.44
CT	9	10	10	10	9.08	0.93	8.42
DE	7	0	10	10	6.84	0.92	6.29
DC	10	10	10	10	10.00	0.93	9.34
FL	7	0	10	10	6.84	0.91	6.23
GA[f]	7	0	10	10	6.84	0.92	6.28
HI[g]	8	0	10	10	7.76	0.91	7.04
ID	7	0	10	10	6.84	0.93	6.33
IL[f]	7	10	10	10	7.24	0.92	6.66
IN[f]	7	0	10	10	6.84	0.93	6.37
IA[h]	7	0	10	10	6.84	0.91	6.21
KS	7	0	10	10	6.84	0.92	6.27
KY	7	0	10	10	6.84	0.92	6.32
LA	7	0	10	10	6.84	0.92	6.31
ME	7	0	10	10	6.84	0.92	6.32
MD[i]	7	10	10	10	7.24	0.92	6.69
MA	8	0	10	10	7.76	0.93	7.25
MI	7	0	10	10	6.84	0.97	6.67
MN	7	0	10	10	6.84	0.94	6.42
MS	7	0	10	10	6.84	0.92	6.32
MO[i]	7	0	10	10	6.84	0.92	6.31
MT[i]	7	10	10	10	7.24	0.96	6.94
NE[f]	7	10	10	10	7.24	0.93	6.73
NV	7	10	0	10	7.04	0.93	6.55
NH	7	0	10	10	6.84	0.93	6.36

(continued)

Table 5.7 (continued)

Juris-diction	Minimum wage provisions[a]				Index	Coverage	Coverage-deflated index
	Wage levels[b]	Inexper-ienced employees[c]	Fines of imprison-ment	Limits on appeal rights[d]			
NJ	7	10	10	10	7.24	0.92	6.68
NM	7	0	10	10	6.84	0.92	6.33
NY	7	0	10	10	6.84	0.92	6.32
NC	7	0	10	10	6.84	0.93	6.36
ND	7	0	10	10	6.84	0.94	6.40
OH[j]	7	0	10	10	6.84	0.93	6.35
OK[f]	7	0	10	10	6.84	0.92	6.28
OR	10	0	10	10	9.60	0.94	8.99
PA	7	0	10	10	6.84	0.92	6.33
RI	7	0	10	10	6.84	0.94	6.40
SC	7	0	10	10	6.84	0.92	6.30
SD	7	0	10	10	6.84	0.93	6.39
TN	7	0	10	10	6.84	0.93	6.36
TX	7	0	10	10	6.84	0.92	6.30
UT	7	0	10	10	6.84	0.94	6.45
VT[f]	8	0	10	10	7.76	0.93	7.20
VA[f]	7	0	10	10	6.84	0.93	6.34
WA	9	10	10	10	9.08	0.95	8.64
WV[f]	7	0	10	10	6.84	0.93	6.39
WI	7	0	10	10	6.84	0.93	6.33
WY	7	0	10	10	6.84	0.92	6.27
CANADA							
Federal	4	10	0	10	4.28	—[e]	—[e]
AB	1	10	0	10	1.52	1	1.52
BC	7	10	0	10	7.04	1	7.04
MB	2	10	0	10	2.44	1	2.44
NB	2	10	0	10	2.44	1	2.44
NF	2	10	0	10	2.44	1	2.44
NT	6[k]	10	0	10	6.12	1	6.12
NS	2	10	0	10	2.44	1	2.44
ON	6	10	0	10[l]	6.12	1	6.12
PE	2	10	0	10	2.44	1	2.44
QC	6	10	0	10	6.12	1	6.12
SK	2	10	0	10	2.44	1	2.44
YT	7	10	0	10	7.04	1	7.04

[a] Table entries are subindex values; index is calculated as a weighted sum of subindex values using 0.92 for wage level; 0.04 for inexperienced employees; and 0.02 for fines and limits on appeal rights.

[b] Subindex values set as follows:

≥US$5.75/Can.$8.05 = 10

 US$5.50 – $5.74/Can$7.70 – Can$8.04 = 9
 US$5.25 – $5.49/Can$7.35 – Can$7.69 = 8
 US$5.00 – $5.24/Can$7.00 – Can$7.34 = 7
 US$4.75 – $4.99/Can$6.65 – Can$6.99 = 6
 US$4.50 – $4.74/Can$6.30 – Can$6.64 = 5
 US$4.25 – $4.49/Can$5.95 – Can$6.29 = 4
 US$4.00 – $4.24/Can$5.60 – Can$5.94 = 3
 US$3.75 – $3.99/Can$5.25 – Can$5.59 = 2
 US$3.50 – $3.74/Can$4.90 – Can$5.24 = 1

States with minimums below the federal minimum and states with no minimum wage provision (AL, AZ, FL, LA, MS, SC, TN) were coded at the federal minimum on the assumption that most firms in the states will affect interstate commerce and therefore be subject to the filed minimum.

Subindex value = 10 if state has subminimum wage provision such that subminimum wage > federal minimum wage.

Canadian data current as of 01/98, see <http://www.gov.ncs.ca/labr/wage_rt.htm>.

[c] Includes learners and apprentices.

[d] In the U.S., the Firm Labor Standards Act (FLSA) requires the Secretary of Labor to request a court injunction when compliance is not forthcoming. See 39 U.S.C. 217. For Canada, see *Canada Labour Code*, Section 251(10).

[e] Not calculated at federal level since employment weights are determined for states or provinces.

[f] State minimum wage subject to minimum employment site:

2 or more: IN, MI (2 or more at anytime during calendar year), VT

4 or more: AR, IL (exclulsive of employer's parent, spouse, child, or immediate family member), NE (not including seasonal workers of 20 or fewer weeks in calendar year), VA (except parent, spouse, or child)

6 or more: WV (located in one location or establishment unless 80% covered by FLSA)

more than 6: GA

10 or fewer: in OK, employees grossing <$100,000 per year with 10 or fewer employees may pay a minimum of $2.00/hr.

[g] An employee earning a guaranteed monthly compensation of $1,250 or more is exempt for minimum wage law.

[h] State minimum is replaced with federal if it is higher than the state minimum.

[i] State law does not curtain dollar minimums; instead state adopts federal minimum by reference.

[j] Minimum wage is $2.80/hr. for employees grossing <$150,000 in annual sales; $3.35/hr. for employees not qualified under 1989 FLSA amendment.

[k] Based on average of Can$6.50 and Can$7.00 = Can$6.75.

[l] Ontario Ministry of Labour, "Employers Guide to Employment Standards Act," at <http://www.gov.on.ca/lab/es/chap6e.htm>.

Table 5.8 Component Scoring for Overtime Index, United States and Canada, December 31, 1998

Jurisdiction	Coding[b]	Limits on appeal rights	Index	Coverage	Coverage-deflated index
	Overtime provisions[a]				
UNITED STATES					
Federal	10	10	10	—[c]	—[c]
AL	10	10	10	0.70	7.01
AK	10	10	10	0.94	9.36
AZ	10	10	10	0.70	6.99
AR	10	10	10	1.00	10.00
CA	10	10	10	0.94	9.41
CO	10	10	10	0.91	9.14
CT	10	10	10	0.93	9.34
DE	10	10	10	0.71	7.06
DC	10	10	10	0.95	9.46
FL	10	10	10	1.00	9.96
GA	10	10	10	0.94	9.40
HI	10	10	10	0.98	9.77
ID	10	10	10	0.84	8.36
IL	10	10	10	0.93	9.29
IN	10	10	10	0.72	7.17
IA	10	10	10	0.70	7.02
KS	10	10	10	0.97	9.75
KY	10	10	10	0.96	9.55
LA	10	10	10	0.71	7.14
ME	10	10	10	0.92	9.19
MD	10	10	10	0.89	8.91
MA	10	10	10	0.90	8.97
MI	10	10	10	1.00	9.96
MN	10	10	10	0.91	9.12
MS	10	10	10	0.72	7.22
MO	10	10	10	0.99	9.90
MT	10	10	10	0.97	9.71
NE	10	10	10	0.69	6.87
NV	10	10	10	0.91	9.09
NH	10	10	10	1.00	10.00
NJ	10	10	10	0.99	9.94
NM	10	10	10	0.93	9.33

Jurisdiction	Overtime provisions[a]		Index	Coverage	Coverage-deflated index
	Coding[b]	Limits on appeal rights			
NY	10	10	10	1.00	9.96
NC	10	10	10	0.90	8.97
ND	10	10	10	0.92	9.16
OH	10	10	10	0.85	8.47
OK	10	10	10	0.70	7.02
OR	10	10	10	0.94	9.42
PA	10	10	10	0.95	9.48
RI	10	10	10	0.96	9.59
SC	10	10	10	0.73	7.31
SD	10	10	10	1.00	10.00
TN	10	10	10	0.72	7.16
TX	10	10	10	0.70	6.98
UT	10	10	10	0.70	7.02
VT	10	10	10	0.91	9.10
VA	10	10	10	0.69	6.89
WA	10	10	10	0.91	9.06
WV	10	10	10	0.98	9.76
WI	10	10	10	0.86	8.57
WY	10	10	10	0.69	6.91
CANADA					
Federal	10.00	10	10.00	0.80	7.99
AB	7.28	10	7.42	0.80	5.86
BC	10.00	10	10.00	1.00	10.00
MB	10.00	10	10.00	0.80	8.00
NB	3.21	10	3.55	1.00	3.21
NF	4.57	10	4.84	0.92	4.21
NT	10.00	10	10.00	0.89	8.89
NS	1.85	10	2.26	0.80	1.48
ON	7.28	10	7.42	0.80	5.80
PE	5.92	10	6.13	0.96	5.67
QC	7.28	10	7.42	0.94	6.87
SK	10.00	10	10.00	0.86	8.64
YT	10.00	10	10.00	0.89	8.89

(continued)

Table 5.8 (continued)

[a] Table entries are subindex values; index is calaculated as a weighted sum of subindex values using 0.95 for coding and 0.05 for limits on appeal rights.

[b] Subindex values coded as follows:

1.5 × reg. rate after 40 hrs. per week = 10
2 × reg. rate after 48 hrs. per week = 8.57
1.5 × reg. rate after 44 hrs. per week = 7.14
1.5 × reg. rate after 48 hrs. per week = 5.71
1.5 × min. wage after 40 hrs. per week = 4.18
1.5 × min. wage after 44 hrs. per week = 2.85
1.5 × min. wage after 48 hrs. per week = 1.42

[c] Not calculated at the federal level since employment weights are determined for states and provinces only.

SOURCE: Canada federal: Canada Labour Code and Regulation.
  Alberta: Employment Standards Code and Regulation.
  British Columbia: Employment Standards Act.
  Manitoba: Employment Standards Act.
  New Brunswick: Minimum Wage Legislation.
  Newfoundland: Labour Standards Act and Regulation.
  Northwest Territory: Employment Standards Act.
  Nova Scotia: Labour Standards Code and Regulations and General Minimum Wage Order (see for exclusions and provisions).
  Ontario: Employment Standards Act and Regulation.
  Prince Edward Island: Employment Standards Act.
  Quebec: The Commission des Normes du Travail. Labor Standards in Quebec.
  Saskatchewan: Labor Standards Act and Regulation.
  Yukon Territory: Employment Standards Act Regulation.

Table 5.9 Component Scoring for Paid Time Off Index, United States and Canada, December 31, 1998

Jurisdiction	Number of holidays	Paid time off or overtime for holidays	Vacation length and pay	Required tenure	Index	Coverage	Coverage-deflated index
UNITED STATES	6.7	0	0	0	1.11	1.00	1.11
Federal							
AL	7.8	0	0	0	1.29	1.00	1.29
AK	6.7	0	0	0	1.11	1.00	1.11
AZ	6.7	0	0	0	1.11	1.00	1.11
AR	6.7	0	0	0	1.11	1.00	1.11
CA	6.7	0	0	0	1.11	1.00	1.11
CO	6.7	0	0	0	1.11	1.00	1.11
CT	6.7	0	0	0	1.11	1.00	1.11
DE	8.9	0	0	0	1.47	1.00	1.47
DC	7.8	0	0	0	1.29	1.00	1.29
FL	6.7	0	0	0	1.11	1.00	1.11
GA	10.0	0	0	0	1.65	1.00	1.65
HI	7.8	0	0	0	1.29	1.00	1.29
ID	7.8	0	0	0	1.29	1.00	1.29
IL	7.8	0	0	0	1.29	1.00	1.29
IN	10.0	0	0	0	1.65	1.00	1.65
IA	7.8	0	0	0	1.29	1.00	1.29
KS	7.8	0	0	0	1.29	1.00	1.29

(continued)

Table 5.9 (continued)

| Jurisdiction | Number of holidays | Paid time off provisions[a] | | Required tenure | Index | Coverage | Coverage-deflated index |
		Paid time off or overtime for holidays	Vacation length and pay				
KY	8.9	0	0	0	1.47	1.00	1.47
LA	10.0	0	0	0	1.65	1.00	1.65
ME	7.8	0	0	0	1.29	1.00	1.29
MD	8.9	0	0	0	1.47	1.00	1.47
MA	7.8	0	0	0	1.29	1.00	1.29
MI	8.9	0	0	0	1.47	1.00	1.47
MN	7.8	0	0	0	1.29	1.00	1.29
MS	7.8	0	0	0	1.29	1.00	1.29
MO	7.8	0	0	0	1.29	1.00	1.29
MT	6.7	0	0	0	1.11	1.00	1.11
NE	8.9	0	0	0	1.47	1.00	1.47
NV	7.8	0	0	0	1.29	1.00	1.29
NH	8.9	0	0	0	1.47	1.00	1.47
NJ	8.9	0	0	0	1.47	1.00	1.47
NM	7.8	0	0	0	1.29	1.00	1.29
NY	7.8	0	0	0	1.29	1.00	1.29
NC	8.9	0	0	0	1.47	1.00	1.47
ND	6.7	0	0	0	1.11	1.00	1.11
OH	6.7	0	0	0	1.11	1.00	1.11
OK	6.7	0	0	0	1.11	1.00	1.11

OR	5.6	0	0	0	0.92	1.00	0.92
PA	7.8	0	0	0	1.29	1.00	1.29
RI	8.9	0	0	0	1.47	1.00	1.47
SC	6.7	0	0	0	1.11	1.00	1.11
SD	7.8	0	0	0	1.29	1.00	1.29
TN	10.0	0	0	0	1.65	1.00	1.65
TX	7.8	0	0	0	1.29	1.00	1.29
UT	7.8	0	0	0	1.29	1.00	1.29
VT	6.7	0	0	0	1.11	1.00	1.11
VA	7.8	0	0	0	1.29	1.00	1.29
WA	7.8	0	0	0	1.29	1.00	1.29
WV	8.9	0	0	0	1.47	1.00	1.47
WI	8.9	0	0	0	1.47	1.00	1.47
WY	5.6	0	0	0	0.92	1.00	0.92
CANADA							
Federal	5.6	10	3.33	10	6.27	1.00	6.27
AB	5.6	10	6.67	6.67	7.61	1.00	7.61
BC	5.6	10	3.33	10	6.27	0.88	5.49
MB	3.3	10	3.33	10	5.89	1.00	5.89
NB	2.2	10	3.33	3.33	5.38	1.00	5.38
NF	1.1	10	3.33	10	5.53	1.00	5.53
NT	5.6	10	3.33	10	6.27	1.00	6.27
NS	2.2	10	3.33	10	5.71	1.00	5.71
ON	4.4	10	3.33	10	6.07	1.00	6.07

(continued)

Table 5.9 (continued)

| Jurisdiction | Number of holidays | Paid time off provisions[a] | | Required tenure | Index | Coverage | Coverage-deflated index |
		Paid time off or overtime for holidays	Vacation length and pay				
PE	1.1	10	3.33	3.33	5.20	1.00	5.20
QC	3.3	10	6.67	6.67	7.23	1.00	7.23
SK	5.6	10	10	6.67	9.11	1.00	9.11
YT	5.6	10	3.33	10	6.27	1.00	6.27

[a] Table entries are subindex values; index is calculated as a weighted sum of subindex values using 0.165 for number of holidays; 0.335 for paid time off or overtime for holidays; 0.45 for vacation length and pay; and 0.05 for required tenure.

Table 5.10 Component Scoring for UI/EI Index, United States and Canada, December 31, 1998

| | Unemployment/employment insurance provisions[a] | | | | |
Jurisdiction	Taxable wage base[b]	Employee tax rate	Replacement rate[c]	Maximum total benefit[d]	Index[e]
UNITED STATES					
Federal	1.7	10	5.0	5.0	6.17
AL	1.7	10	2.0	5.0	5.12
AK	6.7	8.3	1.7	5.0	5.01
AZ	1.7	10	3.3	5.0	5.58
AR	1.7	10	6.7	5.0	6.77
CA	1.7	10	1.7	5.0	5.02
CO	3.3	10	5.0	5.0	6.33
CT	3.3	10	3.3	5.0	5.74
DE	1.7	10	3.3	5.0	5.58
DC	3.3	10	3.3	5.0	5.74
FL	1.7	10	5.0	5.0	6.17
GA	1.7	10	3.3	5.0	5.58
HI	8.3	10	10.0	5.0	8.58
ID	6.7	10	6.7	5.0	7.27
IL	1.7	10	5.0	5.0	6.17
IN	1.7	10	3.3	5.0	5.58
IA	5.0	10	6.7	5.0	7.10
KS	1.7	10	6.7	5.0	6.77
KY	1.7	10	5.0	5.0	6.17
LA	1.7	10	1.7	5.0	5.02
ME	1.7	10	5.0	5.0	6.17
MD	1.7	10	3.3	5.0	5.58
MA	3.3	10	6.7	7.5	7.55
MI	1.7	10	5.0	5.0	6.17
MN	5.0	10	6.7	5.0	7.10
MS	1.7	10	3.3	5.0	5.58
MO	1.7	10	3.3	5.0	5.58
MT	5.0	10	6.7	5.0	7.10
NE	1.7	10	3.3	5.0	5.58
NV	5.0	10	5.0	5.0	6.50
NH	1.7	10	3.3	5.0	5.58
NJ	5.0	10	5.0	5.0	6.50

(continued)

Table 5.10 (continued)

Jurisdiction	Unemployment/employment insurance provisions[a]				
	Taxable wage base[b]	Employee tax rate	Replacement rate[c]	Maximum total benefit[d]	Index[e]
NM	3.3	10	303	5.0	5.74
NY	1.7	10	3.3	5.0	5.58
NC	3.3	10	5.0	5.0	6.33
ND	3.3	10	6.7	5.0	6.93
OH	1.7	10	5.0	5.0	6.17
OK	3.3	10	6.7	5.0	6.93
OR	6.7	10	5.0	5.0	6.67
PA	1.6	10	6.7	5.0	6.76
RI	5.0	10	8.3	5.0	7.66
SC	1.7	10	5.0	5.0	6.17
SD	1.7	10	5.0	5.0	6.17
TN	1.7	10	3.3	5.0	5.58
TX	1.7	10	5.0	5.0	6.17
UT	5.0	10	6.7	5.0	7.10
VT	1.7	10	5.0	5.0	6.17
VA	1.7	10	5.0	5.0	6.17
WA	6.7	10	6.7	7.5	7.89
WV	1.7	10	5.0	5.0	6.17
WI	3.3	10	6.7	5.0	6.93
WY	3.3	10	6.7	5.0	6.93
CANADA[f]	10	1.7	10	10	7.51

[a] Table entries are subindex values; index is calculated as a weighted sum of subindex values using 0.10 for taxable wage base; 0.30 for employee tax rate; 0.35 for average weekly benefit; and 0.25 for minimum total benefit.
[b] Can$1 = US$0.71 (STAT-USA 1998).
[c] Defined as average weekly benefit as a percentage of average weekly wages.
[d] Includes provision for extended benefits.
[e] No coverage-deflated index is calculated because coverage is universal in both countries.
[f] The provisions in all jurisdictions in Canada are identical.

Table 5.11a Component Scoring for Workers' Compensation, United States and Canada, December 31, 1998

| | Workers' compensation provisions[a] | | | | | | | | | | | |
Jurisdiction	Compulsory coverage; private employees (2.1a)	Compulsory coverage; no waivers (2.1b)	No exemptions based on size (2.2)	Farm workers covered (2.4)	Casual workers covered (2.5)	All government workers covered (2.6)	No exemptions; any employee class (2.7)	Employee choice of where to file (2.11)	Coverage for work-related diseases (2.13)	TTB[b] ≥66 2/3% AWW (3.7)	Maximum weekly benefit≥ SAWW[b] (3.8)	PPT[b] definition (3.11)
UNITED STATES												
AL	10	10	0	0	0	0	10	10	10	10	10	10
AK	10	0	10	0	0	0	0	10	10	10	10	10
AZ	10	0	10	10	0	10	0	10	10	10	0	10
AR	10	0	0	0	0	10	0	0	10	10	0	10
CA	10	10	10	10	0	10	10	0	10	10	0	10
CO	10	0	10	10	0	10	0	10	10	10	0	10
CT	10	0	10	10	0	0	0	0	10	10	10	10
DE	10	10	10	0	0	0	0	10	10	10	0	10
DC	10	10	10	10	0	10	10	0	10	10	10	10
FL	10	0	0	0	0	10	0	10	10	10	10	10
GA	10	0	0	0	0	0	0	10	10	10	0	10
HI	10	10	10	10	0	10	0	10	10	10	10	10
ID	10	10	10	0	0	10	0	10	10	10	0	10
IL	10	10	10	0	0	0	0	10	10	10	10	10

(continued)

Table 5.11a (continued)

Jurisdiction	Workers' compensation provisions[a]											
	Compulsory coverage; private employees (2.1a)	Compulsory coverage; no waivers (2.1b)	No exemptions based on size (2.2)	Farm-workers covered (2.4)	Casual workers covered (2.5)	All government workers covered (2.6)	No exemptions; any employee class (2.7)	Employee choice of where to file (2.11)	Coverage for work-related diseases (2.13)	TTB[b] ≥66 2/3% AWW (3.7)	Maximum weekly benefit≥ SAWW[b] (3.8)	PPT[b] definition (3.11)
IN	10	10	10	0	0	10	0	10	10	10	0	10
IA	10	0	10	0	0	10	0	10	10	10	10	10
KS	10	0	10	0	0	10	10	10	10	10	0	10
KY	10	0	10	0	0	10	10	10	10	10	10	10
LA	10	0	10	10	0	0	0	10	10	10	0	10
ME	10	0	10	0	0	10	10	0	10	10	10	10
MD	10	0	10	0	0	10	0	0	10	10	10	10
MA	10	10	10	10	0	0	0	0	10	0	10	10
MI	10	0	10	0	0	10	0	0	10	10	0	10
MN	10	10	10	0	0	0	0	0	10	10	10	10
MS	10	10	0	0	0	0	0	0	10	10	0	10
MO	10	10	0	0	0	10	10	10	10	10	10	10
MT	10	0	10	10	0	10	0	0	10	10	10	10
NE	10	0	10	0	0	10	10	0	10	10	0	10
NV	10	10	10	0	0	10	0	0	10	10	0	10
NH	10	10	10	10	10	10	10	10	10	0	10	10
NJ	0	10	10	10	0	10	10	10	10	10	0	10

NM	10	0	10	10	10	0	10	0	0	0	0	10
NY	10	0	10	10	0	0	0	0	0	10	10	10
NC	10	10	10	10	10	0	10	0	0	0	10	10
ND	10	10	10	10	0	0	10	0	10	10	10	10
OH	10	10	10	10	0	0	10	0	0	10	10	10
OK	10	0	10	10	0	0	10	0	10	10	10	10
OR	10	10	10	10	0	0	10	0	0	10	10	10
PA	10	10	10	10	10	10	0	0	0	0	10	10
RI	10	10	10	10	0	0	0	0	0	0	0	10
SC	10	10	10	10	10	10	0	0	0	10	0	0
SD	10	10	10	10	0	0	0	0	0	0	0	10
TN	10	0	10	10	10	10	0	0	0	10	10	10
TX	10	0	10	10	0	10	0	0	0	10	10	0
UT	10	10	10	10	10	10	10	0	10	10	0	10
VT	10	10	10	10	0	0	0	0	0	0	0	10
VA	10	10	0	10	0	0	0	0	0	10	10	10
WA	10	10	10	10	10	0	10	0	0	10	10	10
WV	10	10	10	10	0	0	10	0	0	0	10	10
WI	10	10	10	10	10	10	10	0	0	10	10	10
WY	10	10	10	0	0	0	0	0	0	10	0	10
CANADA												
AB	10	10	10	10	0	0	0	10	0	10	10	10
BC	10	10	10	10	0	10	10	10	10	10	0	10
MB	10	0	10	0	0	0	0	0	0	10	10	10

(continued)

Table 5.11a (continued)

	Workers' compensation provisions[a]											
Jurisdiction	Compulsory coverage; private employees (2.1a)	Compulsory coverage; no waivers (2.1b)	No exemptions based on size (2.2)	Farm-workers covered (2.4)	Casual workers covered (2.5)	All government workers covered (2.6)	No exemptions; any employee class (2.7)	Employee choice of where to file (2.11)	Coverage for work-related diseases (2.13)	TTB[b] ≥66 2/3% AWW (3.7)	Maximum weekly benefit≥ SAWW[b] (3.8)	PPT[b] definition (3.11)
NB	10	0	0	10	0	0	0	0	10	10	0	10
NF	10	10	10	10	10	10	0	0	10	10	0	10
NT	10	10	10	10	10	10	10	0	10	10	0	10
NS	10	0	0	0	0	0	0	0	10	10	10	10
ON	10	10	10	10	0	10	0	0	10	10	10	10
PE	10	0	10	0	10	10	0	0	10	10	0	10
QC	10	10	10	10	10	10	0	0	10	10	10	10
SK	10	10	10	0	10	10	0	0	10	10	10	10
YT	10	10	10	10	0	10	0	0	10	10	10	10

[a] Table entries are subindex values; index is weighted sum of subindex values. Labels in parentheses are recommendations from *National Commission*. Weights, for recommendations 2.1a, 2.1b, and 3.25a are 0.024; for recommendation 2.11, weight = 0.00 due to lack of data for Canada; for recommendations 3.25b, 3.25c, and 3.25d, weights are 0.008; and for all other recommendations, weights are 0.047. Finally, weights are 0.05 for three appeals provisions.

[b] TTB = temporary total disability benefits; AWW = average weekly wage; SAWW = standard average weekly wage; PPT = permanent part-time; and TTD = temporary total disability.

SOURCE: (U.S.) Burton, John F., and Timothy Schmidle. 1996. *1996 Workers' Compensation Year Book*. Horsham, PA: LRP Publications; (Canada) U.S. Chamber of Commerce 1996. *1996 Analysis of Workers' Compensation Laws*. Washington, D.C.

Table 5.11b Component Scoring for Workers' Compensation, United States and Canada, December 31, 1998

	Workers' compensation provisions[a]												
Juris-diction	PT benefits at least 66 2/3% AWW[b] (3.12)	Max. PT benefits ≥SAWW[b] (3.15)	No time/$ limits on TTD[b] (3.17)	Death benefits ≥66 2/3% AWW[b] (3.21)	Max. death benefits ≥SAWW[b] (3.23)	Continu-ation of death benefits to widow or widower (3.25a)	Lump sum to widow/ widower if remarry (3.25b)	Death benefits for child until age 18 (3.25c)	Death benefits for child until 25 if student (3.25d)	No stat limita-tion med. care/ rehab (4.1)	No time limit on right to Medicare (4.4)	Appeal to internal admin. agency	Internal appeal process
UNITED STATES													
AL	10	10	10	0	10	0	0	0	0	10	10	0	0
AK	10	10	10	10	10	0	10	10	10	10	10	10	0
AZ	10	0	10	0	0	10	0	10	0	10	10	10	0
AR	10	0	10	10	0	10	10	10	10	0	10	10	10
CA	10	0	10	10	0	0	0	0	0	10	0	10	10
CO	10	0	10	10	10	10	10	10	0	10	10	10	10
CT	10	10	10	10	10	10	0	10	0	10	10	10	10
DE	10	0	10	10	0	10	10	10	10	10	10	10	0
DC	10	10	10	0	10	10	0	10	0	10	10	10	10
FL	10	10	10	0	10	10	0	10	0	10	0	10	0
GA	10	0	10	10	0	0	0	10	0	10	10	10	10
HI	10	10	10	0	10	10	10	10	0	10	10	10	10
ID	0	0	10	0	0	0	0	0	0	10	10	10	0

(continued)

Table 5.11b (continued)

	Workers' compensation provisions[a]												
	PT benefits at least 66 2/3% AWW[b] (3.12)	Max. PT benefits ≥SAWW[b] (3.15)	No time/$ limits on TTD[b] (3.17)	Death benefits ≥66 2/3% AWW[b] (3.21)	Max. death benefits ≥SAWW[b] (3.23)	Continuation of death benefits to widow or widower (3.25a)	Lump sum to widow/widower if remarry (3.25b)	Death benefits to child until age 18 (3.25c)	Death benefits to child until 25 if student (3.25d)	No stat. limitation med. care/rehab (4.1)	No time limit on right to Medicare (4.4)	Appeal to internal admin. agency	Internal appeal process
IL	10	10	10	10	10	10	10	10	10	10	10	10	10
IN	10	0	0	10	0	0	10	10	0	10	10	10	10
IA	10	10	10	10	10	10	10	10	10	10	10	10	10
KS	10	0	10	10	0	10	0	10	0	10	0	10	10
KY	10	10	10	0	0	10	10	10	0	10	10	10	10
LA	10	0	10	0	0	10	10	10	0	10	10	10	0
ME	10	10	10	10	10	10	0	10	0	10	0	10	0
MD	10	10	10	10	10	10	10	10	0	10	10	10	0
MA	10	10	0	10	10	10	0	10	10	10	10	10	10
MI	10	0	10	10	0	0	0	10	0	10	10	10	10
MN	10	10	10	0	10	0	0	10	10	10	10	10	10
MS	10	0	0	0	0	0	0	10	0	10	10	10	10
MO	10	10	10	10	10	10	10	10	0	10	0	10	10
MT	10	10	10	10	10	0	0	10	0	10	0	10	10
NE	10	0	10	10	0	10	10	10	10	10	10	10	10
NV	0	0	10	10	0	10	10	10	0	10	10	10	10
NH	10	10	10	0	10	10	0	10	10	10	10	10	10

	C1	C2	C3	C4	C5	C6	C7	C8	C9	C10	C11	C12	C13
NJ	0	10	0	0	0	10	0	10	0	0	0	0	0
NM	10	10	10	10	0	10	10	0	0	10	0	0	0
NY	10	10	10	10	0	10	10	10	0	10	10	0	0
NC	10	10	10	10	0	10	0	0	10	10	10	10	10
ND	10	10	10	10	0	10	0	10	0	10	10	10	10
OH	0	10	10	0	10	10	10	10	10	0	10	0	10
OK	10	10	10	10	0	10	10	10	0	0	10	10	0
OR	10	10	10	10	0	10	0	10	0	0	10	10	10
PA	10	10	10	10	0	10	10	10	10	10	10	10	10
RI	10	10	10	10	0	10	0	10	10	10	0	10	10
SC	10	10	10	10	0	10	10	0	10	10	10	10	10
SD	10	10	10	10	0	10	10	10	0	0	0	0	10
TN	0	0	10	10	0	10	0	10	0	10	0	0	0
TX	10	10	10	10	0	0	10	0	10	10	0	10	0
UT	10	10	10	10	10	10	0	10	10	10	10	10	10
VT	0	0	10	10	0	10	0	0	10	0	10	10	10
VA	10	10	10	10	0	10	0	10	10	10	10	10	10
WA	10	10	10	10	10	10	10	10	10	10	10	10	10
WV	10	10	10	10	0	0	0	0	10	10	10	10	10
WI	10	10	10	10	0	10	0	0	0	0	10	10	10
WY	0	10	10	10	0	0	0	0	0	0	0	0	10
CANADA													
AB	10	10	10	10	0	0	0	0	0	10	10	0	10
BC	10	10	10	10	0	0	0	0	0	10	10	10	10

(continued)

Table 5.11b (continued)

	Workers' compensation provisions[a]												
	PT benefits at least 66 2/3% AWW[b] (3.12)	Max. PT benefits ≥SAWW[b] (3.15)	No time/$ limits on TTD[b] (3.17)	Death benefits ≥66 2/3% AWW[b] (3.21)	Max. death benefits ≥SAWW[b] (3.23)	Continu-ation of death benefits to widow or widower (3.25a)	Lump sum to widow/ widower if remarry (3.25b)	Death benefits to child until age 18 (3.25c)	Death benefits to child until 25 if student (3.25d)	No stat. limita-tion med. care/ rehab (4.1)	No time limit on right to Medicare (4.4)	Appeal to internal admin. agency	Internal appeal process
MB	10	10	0	10	0	0	0	10	0	10	10	10	10
NB	10	0	0	10	10	0	0	0	0	10	10	10	10
NF	10	0	0	10	0	0	0	10	0	10	10	10	10
NT	10	0	10	10	10	10	0	0	0	10	10	10	10
NS	10	10	10	10	10	10	0	10	10	10	10	10	10
ON	10	10	10	0	0	0	0	0	0	10	10	10	10
PE	10	0	10	10	10	10	0	10	0	10	10	10	10
QC	10	10	10	0	0	10	0	0	0	10	10	10	10
SK	10	10	10	10	10	0	0	10	0	10	10	10	10
YT	10	10	0	10	10	10	0	10	0	10	10	10	10

[a] Table entries are subindex values; index is weighted sum of subindex values. Labels in parentheses are recommendations from *National Commission*. Weights, for recommendations 2.1a, 2.1b, and 3.25a are 0.024; for recommendation 2.11, weight = 0.00 due to lack of data for Canada; for recommendations 3.25b, 3.25c, and 3.25d, weights are 0.008; and for all other recommendations, weights are 0.047. Finally, weights are 0.05 for three appeals provisions.

[b] TTB = temporary total disability benefits; AWW = average weekly wage; SAWW = standard average weekly wage; PPT = permanent part-time; and TTD = temporary total disability.

SOURCE: (U.S.) Burton, John F., and Timothy Schmidle. 1996. *1996 Workers' Compensation Year Book*. Hursham, PA: LRP Publications; (Canada) U.S. Chamber of Commerce 1996. *1996 Analysis of Workers' Compensation Laws*. Washington, D.C.

Table 5.11c Component Scoring for Workers' Compensation, United States and Canada, December 31, 1998

Jurisdiction	Provision[a] Level of appeal	Index	Coverage	Coverage-deflated index
UNITED STATES				
AL	0	5.67	0.99	5.64
AK	0	6.64	0.99	6.54
AZ	0	6.02	0.98	5.92
AR	5	5.26	1.00	5.26
CA	5	6.92	0.99	6.86
CO	5	7.07	0.96	6.78
CT	5	7.94	1.00	7.94
DE	5	5.69	0.98	5.60
DC	0	8.65	0.98	8.46
FL	5	5.77	0.95	5.51
GA	0	5.34	0.94	5.04
HI	5	7.91	0.99	7.79
ID	7.5	5.13	0.97	4.97
IL	7.5	7.86	0.99	7.78
IN	5	6.13	0.96	5.90
IA	5	8.10	0.98	7.91
KS	5	6.52	0.91	5.94
KY	5	7.55	0.99	7.44
LA	5	5.38	0.98	5.26
ME	0	7.31	0.98	7.18
MD	2.5	7.27	0.98	7.11
MA	0	7.31	0.98	7.14
MI	5	5.81	0.99	5.75
MN	5	7.20	0.96	6.88
MS	7.5	4.76	0.96	4.55
MO	7.5	7.78	0.98	7.60
MT	5	7.83	0.98	7.67
NE	7.5	7.15	0.97	6.96
NV	5	6.37	0.99	6.32
NH	5	8.85	0.98	8.72
NJ	7.5	4.61	0.97	4.47
NM	5	4.70	0.98	4.60
NY	0	5.89	0.98	5.78

(continued)

Table 5.11c (continued)

Jurisdiction	Provision[a] Level of appeal	Index	Coverage	Coverage- deflated index
NC	5	7.47	0.99	7.37
ND	5	6.95	0.96	6.70
OH	0	8.33	1.00	8.30
OK	5	5.89	0.98	5.75
OR	5	7.70	0.96	7.38
PA	5	7.31	0.99	7.27
RI	5	7.83	0.99	7.77
SC	7.5	6.13	0.96	5.88
SD	5	7.55	0.96	7.25
TN	5	3.51	0.99	3.46
TX	2.5	5.26	0.99	5.23
UT	5	7.86	0.98	7.72
VT	5	7.27	0.98	7.16
VA	0	6.26	0.97	6.05
WA	5	7.78	0.96	7.50
WV	5	8.38	0.99	8.30
WI	7.5	7.86	0.99	7.81
WY	5	4.83	0.96	4.64
CANADA				
AB	10	6.69	0.99	6.62
BC	10	8.58	1.00	8.58
MB	10	6.54	0.99	6.50
NB	10	5.99	0.99	5.95
NF	10	7.25	0.99	7.14
NT	10	8.82	0.99	8.69
NS	10	7.32	0.94	6.86
ON	10	7.64	1.00	7.64
PE	10	7.72	0.98	7.56
QC	10	8.35	0.99	8.30
SK	10	8.66	0.98	8.53
YT	10	8.43	0.99	8.31

[a] Table entries are subindex values; index is weighted sum of subindex values. Labels in parentheses are recommendations from *National Commission*. Weights, for recommendations 2.1a, 2.1b, and 3.25a are 0.024; for recommendation 2.11, weight = 0.00 due to lack of data for Canada; for recommendations 3.25b, 3.25c, and 3.25d, weights are 0.008; and for all other recommendations, weights are 0.047. Finally, weights are 0.05 for three appeals provisions.

SOURCE: (U.S.) Burton, John F., and Timothy Schmidle. 1996. *1996 Workers' Compensation Year Book*. Hursham, PA: LRP Publications; (Canada) U.S. Chamber of Commerce 1996. *1996 Analysis of Workers' Compensation Laws*. Washington, D.C.

Table 5.12 Component Scoring for Collective Bargaining Index, United States and Canada, December 31, 1998

Jurisdiction	Collective bargaining provisions[a]									Coverage-deflated Index
	Statutory protection	Election not required	Unlimited subjects of bargaining	Conciliation during negs compulsory, if req.	Permanent replacements prohibited	First agreement arbitration available	Limits on rights of loser to appeal	Index	Coverage	
UNITED STATES[b]	10	0	0	0	0	0	0	1.5	0.752	1.13
CANADA										
Federal	10	10	0	0	0	10	10	6	—[c]	—[c]
AB	10	0	10	10	0	0	10	6	0.712	4.27
BC	10	10	10	10	10	10	10	10	0.706	7.06
MB	10	10	10	10	0	10	10	9	0.717	6.45
NB	10	10	10	10	0	0	10	8	0.713	5.70
NF	10	10	10	10	0	10	10	9	0.716	6.44
NS	10	0	10	10	0	0	10	6	0.716	4.30
NT	10	10	0	0	0	10	10	6	0.713	4.28
ON	10	10	10	10	0	10	10	9	0.730	6.57
PE	10	10	10	10	0	10	10	9	0.697	6.27
QC	10	10	10	10	10	10	10	10	0.722	7.22
SK	10	10	10	10	0	10	10	9	0.705	6.35
YT	10	10	0	0	0	10	10	6	0.713	4.28

[a] Table entries are subindex values; index is calculated as a weighted sum of subindex values using 0.20 for "Election not required if evidence that majority want union" and "Conciliation during negotiations compulsory"; 0.15 for "Statutory protection" and "Limits on rights of loser for appeal"; and 0.10 for the other three provisions.
[b] States are not listed separately because U.S. federal standards are universal.
[c] Not calculated at federal level since employment weights are determined for provinces.

Table 5.13 Component Scoring for Equal Employment Opportunity and Employment Equity, United States and Canada, December 31, 1998

| | Equal employment opportunity employment equity provisions[a] | | | | | | | | Special situations | | | | | |
| | Protected classes | | | | | | | | | | | Reasonable | | |
Jurisdiction	Race[b]	Gender	National origin	Religion	Age	Sexual preference/ orientation	Disability	Political beliefs	Family leave	Sexual harassment	Equal pay	accommodation for disabled	Limits on rights of appeal	Index
UNITED STATES														
Federal	10	10	10	10	10	0	10	0	10	10	5	10	0	8.35
AL	10	10	10	10	10	0	10	0	10	10	5	10	0	8.35
AK	10	10	10	10	10	0	10	0	10	10	5	10	0	8.35
AZ	10	10	10	10	10	0	10	0	10	10	5	10	0	8.35
AR	10	10	10	10	10	0	10	0	10	10	5	10	0	8.35
CA	10	10	10	10	10	10	10	10	10	10	5	10	0	9.35
CO	10	10	10	10	10	10	10	0	10	10	5	10	0	8.85
CT	10	10	10	10	10	10	10	10	10	10	5	10	0	9.35
DE	10	10	10	10	10	0	10	0	10	10	5	10	0	8.35
DC	10	10	10	10	10	10	10	0	10	10	5	10	0	8.85
FL	10	10	10	10	10	0	10	10	10	10	5	10	0	8.85
GA	10	10	10	10	10	0	10	0	10	10	5	10	0	8.35
HA	10	10	10	10	10	10	10	10	10	10	5	10	0	9.35
ID	10	10	10	10	10	0	10	0	10	10	5	10	0	8.35

(continued)

Table 5.13 (continued)

| Juris-diction | Equal employment opportunity employment equity provisions[a] | | | | | | | | | | | | | |
| | Protected classes | | | | | | | | Special situations | | | | | |
	Race[b]	Gender	National origin	Religion	Age	Sexual preference/ orientation	Disability	Political beliefs	Family leave	Sexual harass-ment	Equal pay	Reason-able accommo-dation for disabled	Limits on rights of appeal	Index
IL	10	10	10	10	10	0	10	0	10	10	5	10	0	8.35
IN	10	10	10	10	10	0	10	0	10	10	5	10	0	8.35
IA	10	10	10	10	10	0	10	0	10	10	5	10	0	8.35
KS	10	10	10	10	10	0	10	10	10	10	5	10	0	8.85
KY	10	10	10	10	10	0	10	10	10	10	5	10	0	8.85
LA	10	10	10	10	10	10	10	0	10	10	5	10	0	8.85
ME	10	10	10	10	10	0	10	0	10	10	5	10	0	8.35
MD	10	10	10	10	10	10	10	10	10	10	5	10	0	9.35
MA	10	10	10	10	10	10	10	0	10	10	5	10	0	8.85
MI	10	10	10	10	10	10	10	0	10	10	5	10	0	8.85
MN	10	10	10	10	10	10	10	0	10	10	5	10	0	8.85
MS	10	10	10	10	10	0	10	10	10	10	5	10	0	8.85
MO	10	10	10	10	10	0	10	0	10	10	5	10	0	8.35
MT	10	10	10	10	10	0	10	10	10	10	5	10	0	8.85
NE	10	10	10	10	10	0	10	0	10	10	5	10	0	8.35
NV	10	10	10	10	10	0	10	0	10	10	5	10	0	8.35
NH	10	10	10	10	10	0	10	0	10	10	5	10	0	8.35

NJ	10	10	10	10	10	10	10	0	10	10	5	10	0	8.85
NM	10	10	10	10	10	10	10	0	10	10	5	10	0	8.85
NY	10	10	10	10	10	10	10	10	10	10	5	10	0	9.35
NC	10	10	10	10	10	0	10	0	10	10	5	10	0	8.35
ND	10	10	10	10	10	0	10	0	10	10	5	10	0	8.35
OH	10	10	10	10	10	10	10	0	10	10	5	10	0	8.85
OK	10	10	10	10	10	0	10	0	10	10	5	10	0	8.35
OR	10	10	10	10	10	0	10	0	10	10	5	10	0	8.35
PA	10	10	10	10	10	10	10	0	10	10	5	10	0	8.85
RI	10	10	10	10	10	10	10	0	10	10	5	10	0	8.85
SC	10	10	10	10	10	0	10	0	10	10	5	10	0	8.35
SD	10	10	10	10	10	0	10	0	10	10	5	10	0	8.35
TN	10	10	10	10	10	0	10	0	10	10	5	10	0	8.35
TX	10	10	10	10	10	0	10	0	10	10	5	10	0	8.35
UT	10	10	10	10	10	10	10	0	10	10	5	10	0	8.35
VT	10	10	10	10	10	0	10	10	10	10	5	10	0	8.85
VA	10	10	10	10	10	10	10	0	10	10	5	10	0	8.85
WA	10	10	10	10	10	0	10	0	10	10	5	10	0	8.85
WV	10	10	10	10	10	10	10	0	10	10	5	10	0	8.35
WI	10	10	10	10	10	0	10	0	10	10	5	10	0	8.85
WY	10	10	10	10	10	0	10	0	10	10	5	10	0	8.35
CANADA														
Federal	10	10	10	10	10	0	10	0	10	10	10	10	10	9.00
AB	10	10	10	10	5	0	10	0	10	10	10	0	10	8.10

(continued)

Table 5.13 (continued)

Jurisdiction	Equal employment opportunity employment equity provisions[a]													
	Protected classes										Special situations			
													Reasonable		
	Race[b]	Gender	National origin	Religion	Age	Sexual preference/ orientation	Disability	Political beliefs	Family leave	Sexual harassment	Equal pay	accommodation for disabled	Limits on rights of appeal	Index
BC	10	10	10	10	5	0	10	10	10	10	10	0	10	8.60
MB	10	10	10	10	5	10	10	10	10	10	10	0	10	9.10
NB	10	10	10	10	5	0	10	0	10	10	10	0	10	8.10
NF	10	10	10	10	5	0	10	10	10	10	10	0	10	8.60
NT	10	10	10	10	10	0	10	0	10	10	10	10	10	9.00
NS	10	10	10	10	5	10	10	10	10	10	10	0	10	9.10
ON	10	10	0	10	10	10	10	10	10	10	10	10	0	8.50
PE	10	10	10	10	5	0	10	10	10	10	10	0	10	8.60
QC	10	10	10	10	5	10	10	0	10	10	10	10	10	9.00
SK	10	10	10	10	5	0	10	10	10	10	10	0	10	8.60
YT	10	10	10	10	10	0	10	0	0	10	10	10	10	8.50

[a] Table entries are subindex values; index is calculated as a weighted sum of the subindices with 0.15 as the weight for race and gender protection; 0.10 for national origin, religion, age, and disability; 0.05 for sexual preference/orientation, political beliefs, family leave, and rights of appeal; 0.04 for reasonable accommodation; and 0.03 for sexual harassment and equal pay provisions.
[b] Includes Aboriginal people and visible minorities.

Table 5.14 Component Scoring for Unjust Discharge Index, United States and Canada, December 31, 1998

| Juris-diction | Unjust discharge provisions[a] | | | | | |
	Discharge prohibited if implicit contract	Handbook exception	Public policy exception	Covenant of good faith exception	Limited to good cause[b]	Index
UNITED STATES						
AL	10	10	10	10	0	3.00
AK	10	10	10	10	0	3.00
AZ	10	10	10	10	0	3.00
AR	10	10	10	0	0	2.00
CA	10	10	10	10	0	3.00
CO	10	10	10	10	0	3.00
CT	10	10	10	10	0	3.00
DE	10	0	0	10	0	1.50
DC	10	10	10	5	0	2.50
FL	10	0	0	5	0	1.00
GA	10	10	0	0	0	1.00
HI	10	10	10	5	0	2.50
ID	10	10	10	10	0	3.00
IL	10	10	10	0	0	2.00
IN	10	0	10	0	0	1.50
IA	10	5	10	10	0	2.75
KS	10	10	10	0	0	2.00
KY	10	5	10	5	0	2.25
LA	10	5	0	5	0	1.25
ME	10	10	5	0	0	1.50
MD	10	10	10	0	0	2.00
MA	10	5	10	10	0	2.75
MI	10	10	10	5	0	2.50
MN	10	10	10	0	0	2.00
MS	10	5	10	5	0	2.25
MO	10	10	10	10	0	3.00
MT	10	10	10	10	10	10.00
NE	10	5	10	5	0	2.25
NV	10	5	10	10	0	2.75
NH	10	10	10	10	0	3.00

(continued)

Table 5.14 (continued)

Juris-diction	Discharge prohibited if implicit contract	Handbook exception	Public policy exception	Covenant of good faith exception	Limited to good cause[b]	Index
			Unjust discharge provisions[a]			
NJ	10	10	10	0	0	2.00
NM	10	10	10	5	0	2.50
NY	10	10	0	0	0	1.00
NC	10	0	10	5	0	2.00
ND	10	5	10	0	0	1.75
OH	10	10	10	5	0	2.50
OK	10	10	10	0	0	2.00
OR	10	10	10	5	0	2.50
PA	10	5	10	0	0	1.75
RI	10	5	5	5	0	1.75
SC	10	10	10	5	0	2.50
SD	10	10	10	0	0	2.00
TN	10	0	10	5	0	2.00
TX	10	10	10	5	0	2.50
UT	10	10	10	5	0	2.50
VT	10	10	10	5	0	2.50
VA	10	5	10	5	0	2.25
WA	10	10	10	0	0	2.00
WV	10	10	10	5	0	2.50
WI	10	10	10	0	0	2.00
WY	10	10	10	10	0	3.00
CANADA[c]						
Federal	0	0	0	0	10	7.00

[a] Table entries are subindex values; index is calculated as a weighted sum of the subindex with 0.70 for limited to "good cause"; 0.10 for public policy and covenant of good faith exceptions; and 0.05 for implicit contract and handbook exceptions.
[b] Limited, except for misconduct, incompetence, or negligence.
[c] The provisions in all jurisdictions in Canada are identical.

Table 5.15a Component Scoring for Occupational Safety and Health, United States and Canada, December 31, 1998

	Subject to general duty clause	Warrant can be demanded prior to entry	Maximum penalty for willful violation of statute[c]	Max. penalty for serious violation of statute[c]	Maximum penalty for willful violation of OSHA[c]	Repeat violation penalties subj. to 10x increase	Penalty for 1st offense, willful violation causing death	Penalty for 2nd offense, willful violation causing death	Daily penalty assessed for failing to abate hazard[d]	Reduction in penalties for firms ≤ 250 employees	Reduction for written health & safety programs
UNITED STATES[b]	10	0	1.7	1.7	6.7	10	0	3.33	6.7	10	10
CANADA											
Federal	0	10	3.33	0	0	0	10	0	0	0	0
AB	0	10	0	0	10	0	0	0	10	0	0
BC	0	10	10	0	0	0	0	0	0	0	0
MA	0	10	1.7	0	3.33	0	0	0	3.3	0	0
NB	0	10	0	0	0	0	0	0	0	0	0
NF	0	10	0	0	0	0	0	0	1.7	0	0
NW	0	10	1.7	0	0	0	0	0	0	0	0
NS	0	10	0	0	0	0	0	0	1.7	0	0
ON	0	10	10	0	0	0	0	0	0	0	0
PE	0	10	0	0	0	0	0	0	1.7	0	0
QC	0	10	3.33	0	5[e]	0	0	0	0	0	0

Occupational safety and health provisions[a]

Penalty for

(continued)

Table 5.15a (continued)

| SK | 0 | 10 | 0 | 0 | 1.7 | 0 | 0 | 0 | 1.7 | 0 | 0 |
| YT | 0 | 10 | 1.7 | 0 | 5 | 0 | 0 | 0 | 1.7 | 0 | 0 |

[a] Table entries are subindex values for each provision; index is weighted sum of subindices with the five recordkeeping categories using weights of 0.02; and the remaining 17 categories using 0.053, except for limits on appeal, which use 0.052.

[b] All U.S. states subject to federal statute.

[c] Coding: ≥ \$100,000 = 10; \$80,000–\$99,999 = 8.33; \$ 60,000–\$79,999 = 6.7; \$40,000–\$59,999 = 5.0; \$20,000–\$39,999 = 3.33; \$1,000–\$19,999 = 1.7; no penalty = 0 (all \$ amounts are domestic).

[d] Coding: ≥ \$10,000 = 10; \$8,000–\$9,999 = 8.3; \$6,000–7,999 = 6.7; \$4,000–\$5,999 = 5.0; \$2,000–\$3,999 = 3.3; \$1–\$1,999 = 1.7; no time = 0 (all \$ amounts are domestic).

[e] QC: Maximum subsequent fine is \$50,000 for corporations and \$2,000 for individuals.

Table 5.15b Component Scoring for Occupational Safety and Health, United States and Canada, December 31, 1998

Jurisdiction	Penalty reduction if absence of violations	Record-keeping exemptions for small firms	State\provinces may set stricter standards	Occ. safety comm. or representative required	Maximum imprisonment possible[c]	Max. penalty for penalty for contravening without directives[d]	Max. contravention by anyone[e]	Maximum penalty, minor offense[f]	Additional fines possible	Daily penalty for nonabatement of second hazard[e]	Limits on appeal rights	Index
				Occupational safety and health provisions[a]								
UNITED STATES[b]	10	10	10	0	0	0	0	0	0	0	0	3.13
CANADA												
Federal	0	0	10	10	10	3.33	10	5	10	0	0	4.33
AB	0	0	10	0[g]	8	10.00	0	0	0	0	0	3.07
BC	0	0	10	10[h]	4	3.33	3.3	0	0	5	10	3.20
MA	0	0	10	10	6	0	0	0	0	0	10	3.13
NB	0	0	10	10	0	0	0	0	0	0	10	2.11
NF	0	0	10	0	6	1.70	0	0	0	0	10	2.08
NT	0	0	10	0	8	1.70[i]	0	0	0	0	10	2.18
NS	0	0	10	0	8	1.70	0	0	0	0	10	2.18
ON	0	0	10	10	8	3.33	0	0	0	0	10	3.24
PE	0	0	10	0	2	1.70	0	0	0	0	10	1.87
QC	0	0	10	0	8	1.70	1.7	0	0	0	10	2.63
SK	0	0	10	10[j]	10	1.70	0	0	0	1.7	10	3.00
YT	0	0	10	10	0	3.33	0	0	10[k]	0	10	3.17

(continued)

[a] Table entries are subindex values for each provision; index is weighted sum of subindices with the five recordkeeping categories using weights of 0.02; and the remaining 17 categories using 0.053, except for limits on appeal, which use 0.052.

[b] All U.S. states subject to federal statute.

[c] Coding: 24 months = 10; 12 months = 8; 6 months = 6; 3 months = 4; 1 month = 2; no imprisonment = 0.

[d] Coding: ≥$100,000 = 10; $80,000–$99,999 = 8.33; $ 60,000–$79,999 = 6.7; $40,000–$59,999 = 5.0; $20,000–$39,999 = 3.33; $1,000–$19,999 = 1.7; no penalty = 0 (all $ amounts are domestic).

[e] Coding: ≥ $10,000 = 10; $8,000–$9,999 = 8.3; $6,000–7,999 = 6.7; $4,000–$5,999 = 5.0; $2,000–$3,999 = 3.3; $1–$1,999 = 1.7; no time = 0 (all $ amounts are domestic).

[f] Minor offenses refer to acts such as: failure to post information, failure of keep records, not providing sanitary or personal facilities, failure to cooperate with safety/health persons, and failing to report accident. Source: *A Guide to the Canada Labor Code, Occupational Safety and Health Canada*, L31-87, 1992. Coded as in note d.

[g] AB leaves committee up to discretion of the minister of labor.

[h] BC allows companies that have a low hazardous rating ("C") to be exempt up to 50 employees.

[i] NT: Employees can be fined up to $1,000 and six months in prison. If employer is guilty, every employee involved could be fined $500 and sentenced to one month in jail.

[j] SK: Committees are mandatory in businesses with > ten workers.

[k] YT: Flat rate minimum for continuing offenses (not daily). Each offense gets fined: Regulation violation: $1,500 for first, $2,500 for subsequent; for order violation: $1,750 first, $2,750 subsequent; and for work stop violation: $2,000 first, $3,000 subsequent.

Table 5.16 Component Scoring for Advance Notice of Plant Closings and Large Scale Layoffs, United States and Canada, December 31, 1998

Jurisdiction	Advanced notice/group termination provisions[a]								Index
	Number of employees	Max. time period until layoffs	Advanced notice required	Notice to Labor Minister/govt.	Notice to affected employees	Notice to union	Severance pay	Limits on appeal	
UNITED STATES[b]	3.3	6.7	5	10	10	10	0	0	5.03
CANADA									
Federal	3.3	6.7	10	10	0	0	10	10	5.53
AB	0	0	0	0	0	0	0	0	0.00
BC	3.3	3.3	7.5	10	10	10	10	10	7.89
MB	3.3	6.7	7.5	10	10	10	0	10	6.03
NB	6.7	6.7	2.5	10	10	10	0	10	5.71
NF	3.3	6.7	7.5	10	10	0	0	10	5.03
NT	6.7	6.7	5	10	0	0	0	10	3.21
NS	10	6.7	7.5	10	10	0	0	10	6.37
ON	3.3	6.7	7.5	10	10	0	10	10	7.03
PE	0	0	0	0	0	0	0	0	0.00
QC	10	10	7.5	10	0	0	0	10	4.50
SK	10	6.7	5	10	10	10	0	10	6.87
YT	6.7	6.7	5	10	10	0	0	10	5.21

[a] Table entries are subindex values; index is weighted sum of subindices using 0.20 for number of employees, advanced notice required, notice to affected employees, and severance pay; 0.10 for notice to union; 0.05 for limits on appeal; 0.04 for maximum time period; and 0.01 for notice to Labor Minister.
[b] All U.S. states subject to federal statute.

Notes

1. This chapter summarizes the results for the labor standards computations for the United States and Canada as of December 31, 1998. Readers interested in the raw data on which the indices are based are encouraged to go to the following Web site: <www.upjohninstitute.org/BlockRoberts>.

2. Employment data are for 1995, which was the last full year available for both countries. In addition, the employment-weighted average for Canada excludes the federal jurisdiction. To separate the federal jurisdiction would require us to subtract from each province's employment estimate the number of employed persons in the province who are employed in an industry in the federal jurisdiction. At this stage, our data will not permit us to make such a calculation. It is necessary to make such an adjustment for the United States because in the United States, all employees in a state are covered by the labor standard in the state if that labor standard is higher than the federal standard. If it is lower, the federal standard prevails unless the employer is one of the very few that do not affect interstate commerce.

3. The above discussion presumes that each standard is equally important. It is possible, however, that the value of a standard might differ across different types of users, such as firms, unions, policymakers, or researchers. See the appendix Table 5.11A, "Scenarios Using Alternative Weighting of Standards," for examples of scenarios that a policymaker concerned about attracting industry or a firm making a location decision might examine in addition to the basic index.

4. The assumption in summing the indices of the standards is that each of the standards is equally important. Other assumptions may also be reasonable.

5. Minimum wage levels, denominated in domestic dollars, are generally higher in Canada as of December 31, 1998, than in the United States. The federal minimum wage in the United States was raised to US$5.15 as of September 1, 1997. Eight states and the District of Columbia have enacted minimum wage rates higher than the federal rate, with the highest being $6.50 per hour in Oregon. Canadian nominal minimum wage rates range from Can$5.00 in Alberta to Can$7.15 in British Columbia.

6. See web site <http://iaita.doc.gov/exchange> for underlying data.

7. For the purposes of this study, in computing coverage we did not consider the number of employees in the two countries who might be exempt from coverage of the overtime provision due to executive, professional, or managerial status. See, for example, U.S. Department of Labor (2001). Whether such employees are exempt from overtime is based on an individualized study of the nature of their work, and such estimates are unavailable for the United States. Therefore, not considering these provisions maintains similarity in the criteria across the two countries, but it should not affect the rankings if the percentage of executive, professional, and managerial employees is comparable across jurisdictions.

8. It is possible, of course, that regardless of whether employers directly pay the nominal cost of unemployment insurance, the burden is actually shifted to

employees in the form of forgone earnings. Then, weighting the index to account for direct employee payments may underestimate the advantage for Canada relative to the United States because all costs are actually borne by employees. Adding a separate provision for employee payment is simply a decomposition of the costs borne by all employees. Nevertheless, given our method of limiting the index to statutory provisions, consistency requires that we take separate account of this provision.

9. These values are not shown, although they can be computed from Table 5.16. The nondeflated, unweighted average is the average of all jurisdictions, including the federal jurisdiction, except Alberta and PEI. The coverage-deflated, employment-weighted average is the average of all jurisdictions except Alberta, PEI, and the federal jurisdiction. The federal jurisdiction is excluded because coverage rates are computed by province. See Chapter 4.

Chapter 5 Appendix

Alternative Weighting

One concern with the study is that the results reported in Chapter 5 might be an artifact of the provision weights. Although we chose the weighting schemes as reported in the body of Chapter 4 to reflect our assessment of the spirit of each standard, we acknowledge that other weighting schemes could be equally plausible. To test the robustness of the results, we simulated three cases: a *base case*, an *essential provisions case*, and a *smoothing case*. The base case is the set of weights described in Chapter 4, based on our best judgment of the importance of the various provisions to the purpose of the standard.

The essential provisions case reweights the provisions so that only the provisions that are essential to the purpose of each labor standard are positively weighted. For seven of the standards (advance notice, collective bargaining, minimum wage, overtime, paid time off, UI/EI, and unjust discharge), we reduced the number of provisions considered in each standard to 2 or fewer. We reduced the labor standard for EEO/EE to 8 provisions; that for occupational safety and health to 5; and that for workers' compensation to 10.

The smoothing case smooths the weights across provisions by reweighting the most important provisions by 80 percent of their former value and spreading the remainder (1 minus the sum of the new weights for the important provisions) equally across the remaining provisions.

Tables 5.1A through 5.10A show the weights for all three cases.

Table 5.1A   Minimum Wage: Alternative Weights

Provision	Base	Essential purpose	Smoothed
Minimum wage level[a]	0.92	1.0	0.736
Subminimum wage	0.04		0.088
Fines, imprisonment	0.02		0.088
Right of appeal of agency decision	0.02		0.088

[a] As of April 1, 1997.

Table 5.2A Overtime: Alternative Weights

Provision	Base	Essential purpose	Smoothed
Overtime	0.95	1.0	0.76
Limits on rights of appeal of agency decisions	0.05		0.24

Table 5.3A Paid-Time Off: Alternative Weights

Provision	Base	Essential purpose	Smoothed
Holidays	0.165		0.132
Pay or overtime[a]	0.335	0.5	0.268
Vacation length and pay coding	0.45	0.5	0.36
Eligibility	0.05		0.24

[a] Pay for holidays taken or overtime for holidays worked.

Table 5.4A Unemployment or Employment Insurance: Alternative Weights

Provision	Base	Essential purpose	Smoothed
Taxable wage base	0.1		0.1
Employee tax rate	0.3		0.3
Average weekly benefit[a]	0.35	0.5	0.35
Maximum total benefit	0.25	0.5	0.25

[a] As a percentage of average weekly wages.

Table 5.5A Workers' Compensation: Alternative Weights

Provision	Base	Essential purpose	Smoothed
Compulsory coverage for private employment	0.024	0.1	0.039
No waivers permitted	0.024	0.1	0.039
No exemption based on firm size	0.047		0.038
Farmworkers covered	0.047		0.038
Casual and household workers covered	0.047		0.038
Mandatory government worker coverage	0.047		0.038
No exemptions based on employee class	0.047		0.038
Employee choice over where to file	0.000		0.039
Coverage for all work-related diseases	0.047		0.038
Temporary total disabiliy (TTD) benefits ≥ 66 2/3% wages (subject to maximum)	0.047	0.1	0.038
Maximum TTD benefit at least 100% standard averge weekly wages (SAWW)	0.047	0.1	0.038
Retain prevailing PT definition	0.047		0.038
PT benefits ≥ 66 2/3% wages (s.t. maximum)	0.047	0.1	0.038
Maximum part-time benefit at least 100% SAWW	0.047	0.1	0.038
Benefit duration = disability duration	0.047	0.1	0.038
Death benefits ≥ 66 2/3% wages	0.047	0.1	0.038
Maximum death benefit at least 100% SAWW	0.047	0.1	0.038
Benefits to widow(er)	0.024		0.039
Lump sum to widow(er) on remarriage	0.008		0.039
Benefits to dependent child until 18	0.008		0.039
Benefits to dependent child until 25 if student	0.008		0.039
No statutory $ limit on medical or rehab. services	0.047	0.1	0.038
No time limit on right to medical or rehab. services	0.047		0.038
Right of appeal			
Internal first level agency	0.05		0.04
Internal appeal process	0.05		0.04
Levels of appeal beyond first	0.05		0.04

Table 5.6A Collective Bargaining: Alternative Weights

Provision	Base	Essential purpose	Smoothed
Statutory protection for collective bargaining	0.15	0.5	0.15
Election requirements[a]	0.2	0.5	0.20
Unlimited subjects of bargaining	0.1		0.10
Conciliation rights[b]	0.2		0.20
Striker permanent replacements prohibited	0.1		0.10
First-agreement arbitration available	0.1		0.10
Limits on rights of loser to appeal	0.15		0.15

[a] The jurisdiction's subindex value is coded as 10 if the provision is in effect; 0 otherwise.

[b] Election is not required if there is evidence that a majority support the union.

Table 5.7A Equal Employment Opportunity and Employment Equity: Alternative Weights

Provision	Base	Essential purpose	Smoothed
Race, visible minorities, Aboriginal peoples	0.15	0.125	0.12
Gender	0.15	0.125	0.12
National origin or ancestry	0.10	0.125	0.069
Religion	0.10	0.125	0.069
Age	0.10	0.125	0.069
Sexual preference or orientation	0.05	0.125	0.069
Disability	0.10	0.125	0.069
Political beliefs, organization memberships	0.05	0.125	0.069
Family leave	0.05		0.069
Sexual harassment	0.03		0.069
Equal pay	0.03		0.069
Reasonable accommodation for disabled employees	0.04		0.069
Limits on rights of appeal	0.05		0.069

Table 5.8A Unjust Discharge: Alternative Weights

Provision	Base	Essential purpose	Smoothed
Discharge prohibited if implicit contract	0.05		0.11
Handbook exception	0.05		0.11
Public policy exception	0.10		0.11
Covenant-of-good-faith exception	0.10		0.11
Limited[a]	0.70	1.0	0.56

[a] Coded as 10 if the provision is in effect; 0 otherwise.

Table 5.9A Occupational Safety and Health: Alternative Weights

Provision	Base	Essential purpose	Smoothed
Subject to general duty clause	0.02		0.056
Inspection warrant required	0.053	0.17	0.042
Maximum penalty for a willful violation	0.053	0.17	0.042
Maximum penalty for a serious violation	0.053	0.16	0.042
Maximum penalty for a willful repeat violation	0.053	0.16	0.042
Repeat violation penalties	0.053		0.042
Willful violation causing death			
Penalty for 1st offense	0.053	0.17	0.042
Penalty for 2nd offense	0.053		0.042
Penalty for failing to abate a hazard	0.053	0.17	0.042
Reduction in penalties for firms			
With less than 250 employees	0.02		0.056
With written health and safety program	0.02		0.056
With no violations during a specified time	0.02		0.056
Record keeping exemptions for small firms or specified industries	0.02		0.056
Stricter standards than federal	0.053		0.042
Occupational safety committee or represenative required	0.053		0.042
Maximum imprisonment possible	0.053		0.042
Maximum penalty for contravening direction of safety officer or inspector	0.53		0.042
Maximum penalty for any contravention by anyone	0.053		0.042

(continued)

Table 5.9A (continued)

Provision	Base	Essential purpose	Smoothed
Maximum penalty for minor offenses	0.053		0.042
Additional fines possible	0.053		0.042
Penalty for failing to abate a second hazard	0.053		0.042
Limits on appeal of agency decisions	0.052		0.042

Table 5.10A Advance Notice of Plant Closings or Large-Scale Layoffs: Alternative Weights

Provision	Base	Essential purpose	Smoothed
Number of employees	0.20		0.16
Maximum time in which layoffs must occur	0.04		0.09
Advanced notice required	0.20	1.0	0.16
Notice to minister of labor or government	0.01		0.09
Notice to affected employee	0.20		0.16
Notice to union	0.10		0.09
Severance pay	0.20		0.16
Limits on appeal of agency decisions	0.05		0.09

The discussion in Chapter 5 presumes that each standard is equally important. It is possible, however, that the value of a standard might differ across different types of users, such as firms, unions, policymakers, or researchers. Table 5.11A gives two examples of scenarios that a policymaker concerned about attracting industry, or a firm making a location decision, might examine in addition to the basic index. Consider, for example, the interests of two types of firms: a software development firm and a small-niche steel manufacturing plant. We constructed a scenario for each of these firms by simply changing the standards such that they continue to sum to 10, but are no longer weighted equally. In the software case, we assume that the industry hires contract workers on a project basis, that the workforce is not unionized, and that workers are paid well above the minimum wage. Thus minimum wage, paid time off, collective bargaining, overtime, and advance notice are excluded from the analysis. We weight the remaining five standards equally.

In the case of the small steel-manufacturing plant, the plant expects to pay all its employees a wage rate above the minimum so that standard does not apply, but the remaining standards do. However, the manufacturer has particular

Table 5.11A   Scenarios Using Alternative Weighting of Standards

	Scenario					
Jurisdiction/ index	Basic index	Deflated basic index	Software example	Deflated software	Small mfg. example	Deflated small mfg. example
U.S. unweighted average	52.24	49.42	52.13	49.92	46.95	44.62
Canada unweighted average	64.10	60.55	64.71	60.55	65.28	55.93
U.S. weighted average	51.78	49.64	51.38	49.64	51.76	51.01
Canada weighted average	67.62	63.16	65.63	63.16	65.27	64.29

concerns: specifically, it is concerned about safety, because it uses a dangerous production process, and collective bargaining, because most plants in this industry are organized. Therefore, in this case, workers' compensation, occupational safety and health, and collective bargaining are given twice the weights of the remaining six standards.

The unweighted and weighted averages in the table show that the U.S. average index improves slightly relative to Canada for the software producers, but declines considerably for the small manufacturer for both the values of the index and the rankings. Not shown in the table, but available from the authors upon request, are the relative rankings of the states/provinces in the two scenarious, which change somewhat.

6
Summary and Conclusions

This study takes the first step toward evaluating the differences in labor standards between Canada and the United States by creating a means to measure the strength of 10 labor standards in the two countries. Specifically, each standard is evaluated using an ordinal scale. Absent provisions are assigned a score of 0 and the strongest provision a score of 10. Provisions of intermediate strength are assigned intermediate values in accordance with the number of possible categories in the provision.

Taking the 10 standards as a group, assuming that all standards are equally important and that the internal scalings of the standards are identical, the results indicate that Canadian labor standards are higher than U.S. labor standards. The sum of the basic unweighted Canadian indices is 64.30, while the sum of the basic U.S. unweighted indices is 52.24. The sum of the basic employment-weighted Canadian indices is 65.27, while the sum of the basic employment-weighted U.S. indices is 51.91.

The superiority of the overall level of Canadian labor standards vis-à-vis U.S. labor standards is confirmed by the ranking analysis. Of the 12 Canadian provinces and territories, 6 are among the 10 highest ranked in the study. Similarly, the average Canadian ranking is 14.92, while the average U.S. ranking is 36.02. This difference is significant at the 0.001 level. Thus, a broad-based overview of the labor standards in the two countries suggests that the conventional wisdom is correct— Canadian labor standards are indeed higher than U.S. labor standards.

An examination of the rankings on individual labor standards generally confirms the conclusions from the two broad-based analyses. Nevertheless, in some standards the United States is superior to Canada. The ranks on the minimum wage, overtime, and occupational safety and health standards in the United States are higher than those in the Canadian jurisdictions. Moreover, the differences in the ranks between the two countries in the equal employment opportunity and employment equity standard is insignificant, supporting the view that the two countries are equal with respect to this standard. Significant differences in favor of Canada appear in standards involving paid time off, unemployment or employment insurance, workers' compensation, collective bargaining, unjust discharge, and advance notice.

Canadian jurisdictions also demonstrate greater variation than do the jurisdictions in the United States. This is because the Canadian constitutional system gives the provinces far more authority to legislate than the U.S. constitution does to individual states in areas in which the U.S. federal government chooses to regulate. Thus in the United States, if the federal government chooses to regulate in an area, federal law creates a floor for all states, resulting in uniformity.

CAVEATS

Four important caveats should be noted when analyzing this work.

First, the creation of the indices depends largely on the selection of provisions within each labor standard, and on the weights given to the various provisions. Excluded provisions or different weights would result in different indices. We believe our weights are reasonable, but other weighting schemes may also be reasonable. By making the data publicly available, this study allows other researchers to revise the weighting scheme using different assumptions. We address this in Chapter 4 by using multiple scenarios. But also, because the data are available, other researchers can address this caveat by using the same method but applying different weights.

Second, we define labor standards quite narrowly, limiting our definition to those standards that appear in both countries and that directly affect the employer-employee relationship in both countries. We exclude such issues as social security, child labor, and health insurance even though, to some extent, these have implications for employment relations.

Third, our summing of the indices and the rankings assumes that each of the standards is equally important. It is quite likely, however, that not all standards will be equally important to all firms and all employees. If a firm produces a labor-intensive product, and that firm pays relatively low wages, the employees and management of that firm may be most concerned about such standards as the minimum wage, overtime, and paid time off. High-wage, capital-intensive employers may be most concerned about standards that may be perceived as constraining hiring, such as equal employment opportunity and employment equity. High-wage, unionized employees may be unconcerned about minimum wage and overtime standards. Researchers can address such concerns by using the publicly available data to link specific standards to specific industries. In the appendix to Chapter 5, for example, we relax the equality assumption. Moreover, as they can with the internal weights, researchers using the publicly available data can alter the importance given to each standard.

Fourth, before we look beyond the United States and Canada, we must keep in mind that in comparing the United States and Canada we are comparing two countries that have many similarities. Any attempt to extend this work as a template for studying other countries must take into account any differences in such measures as the size of the informal economy in developing countries (ILO 1995), the importance of collective bargaining as a standard-setting mechanism in European countries, and the fact that not all countries have the same labor market problems, suggesting that the baseline standards are not the same in all countries.[1]

Nevertheless this U.S.-Canada comparison is a complex study because of the large number of jurisdictions in the two countries that could promulgate labor standards. In other words, while this study compares only two countries, at the same time it compares 63 political jurisdictions. In that sense, it simulates a multicountry comparison if the countries generally promulgate standards at the national level.

IMPLICATIONS

Despite these caveats, the results presented in this study are generally consistent with the conventional wisdom: the overall level of labor standards in Canada is higher than the overall level of labor standards in the United States. These results, then, provide some validation of the method. The method generates the expected results.

We hope that this database will be used to answer questions that, to a large extent, have not been researched. Do labor standards affect

trade flows between the United States and Canada? Are there differences in economic growth, investment, and employment that can be
linked to the level of labor standards? Put simply, do labor standards
matter, and, if so, how much? More than anything else, our goal with
this study is to move the debate about international labor standards
from a reliance on assertion, theory, and morality to a reliance on analysis and results.

Note

1. For example, while guest workers represent an important labor market issue in the
   emerging countries of Asia (Lee 1997), they are much less of an issue in the
   United States.

References

Abramson, Jill, and Steven Greenhouse. 1997. "Fight Over Trade Bill Show-cases Labor's Growing Political Muscle." *The New York Times*, November 12.

Adams, George W. 1995. "Review of Recent Amendments to Ontario's Labour Legislation." Supplement to *Canadian Labour Law,* Second Edition by George W. Adams. Aurora, Ontario: Canada Law Book.

————. 1997. *Canadian Labour Law*, 2nd Ed. Aurora, Ontario: Canada Law Book, (May).

Adams, Roy J. 1993. "The Role of the State in Industrial Relations." In *Research Frontiers in Industrial Relations,* D. Lewin, O. Mitchell, and P. Sherer, eds. Madison, Wisconsin: Industrial Relations Research Association.

Addison, John, Douglas Fox, and Christopher Ruhm. 1995. "Trade and Displacement in Manufacturing." *Monthly Labor Review* 118(6): 58–66.

Aggarwal, Mita. 1995a. "International Trade, Labor Standards, and Labor Market Conditions: An Evaluation of the Linkages." Working Paper 95-06-C. U.S. International Trade Commission, Office of Economics.

————. 1995b. "International Trade and the Role of Labor Standards." *International Economic Review* 8: 22–30.

Appelbaum, Eileen, and Rosemary Batt. 1994. *The New American Workplace*. Ithaca, New York: ILR Press.

Armah, Bartholomew. 1994. "Impact of Trade on Service Sector Employment: Implications for Women and Minorities." *Contemporary Economic Policy* 12(1): 67–78.

Ballantyne, Duncan S., and Christopher J. Mazingo. 1999. *Measuring Dispute Resolution Outcomes: A Literature Review with Implications for Workers' Compensation*. Cambridge, Massachusetts: Workers Compensation Research Institute, April.

Barber, Lionel. 1997. "Labour to Pledge a Fresh Start in Europe; Blair Is Preparing to Sign the Social Chapter of the EU's Maastricht Treaty in Six Weeks." *Financial Times,* May 5, p. 8.

Basu, Kaushik, and Pahm Hoang Van. 1998. "The Economics of Child Labor." *The American Economic Review* 88(3): 412–427.

Beach, Charles M., and George A. Slotsve. 1996. *Are We Becoming Two Societies?* Toronto, Ontario: C.D. Howe Institute.

Bednarzik, Robert. 1993. "An Analysis of U.S. Industries Sensitive to Trade: 1982–87." *Monthly Labor Review* 116(2): 15–31.

Ben-David, Dan. 1993. "Equalizing Exchange: Trade Liberalization and Income Convergence." *Quarterly Journal of Economics* 108(3): 653–679.

Blackburn, McKinley L., and David E. Bloom. 1993. "The Distribution of Family Income: Measuring and Explaining Changes in the 1980s for Canada and the United States." In *Small Differences that Matter,* David Card and Richard Freeman, eds. Chicago, Illinois: University of Chicago Press, pp. 233–265.

Blank, Rebecca. 1994. "Does a Larger Social Safety Net Mean Less Economic Flexibility?" In *Working under Different Rules,* R. Freeman, ed. New York: Russell Sage Foundation, pp. 157–187.

Blank, Rebecca, and Maria Hanratty. 1993. "Responding to Need: A Comparison of Social Safety Nets in Canada and the United States." In *Small Differences that Matter*, David Card and Richard Freeman, eds. Chicago, Illinois: University of Chicago Press, pp.191–231.

Block, Richard N. 1978a. "The Impact of Seniority Provisions on the Manufacturing Quit Rate." *Industrial and Labor Relations Review* 31(4): 474–488.

———. 1978b. "Job Changing and Negotiated Nonwage Provisions." *Industrial Relations* 17(3): 296–307.

———. 1992. "The Legal and Institutional Framework for Employment Security in the United States: An Overview." In *Employment Security and Labor Market Flexibility: An International Perspective*, Kazutoshi Koshiro, ed. Detroit, Michigan: Wayne State University Press, pp. 127–148.

———. 1994. "Reforming U.S. Labor Law and Collective Bargaining: Some Proposals Based on the Canadian Industrial Relations System." In *Restoring the Promise of American Labor Law*, S. Friedman, R. Hurd, R. Oswald, and R. Seeber, eds. Ithaca, New York: ILR Press, pp. 250–259.

———. 1996. "NAFTA, Collective Bargaining, and Employment Adjustments in the United States and Canada." In *Policy Choices: Free Trade Among NAFTA Nations*, Karen Roberts and Mark Wilson, eds. East Lansing, Michigan: Michigan State University Press, pp. 217–234.

———. 1997a. "Rethinking the National Labor Relations Act and Zero-Sum Labor Law; An Industrial Relations View." *Berkeley Journal of Employment and Labor Law* 18(1): 30–55.

———. 1997b. "Collective Bargaining and the Courts: An Empirical Analysis of Judicial Review of NRLB Decision and Arbitration Awards." *Proceedings of the 25th Annual Conference of the National Center for the Study of Collective Bargaining in Higher Education and the Professions.* Baruch College, New York, April, pp. 176–191.

Block, Richard N., John Beck, and Daniel H. Kruger. 1996. *Labor Law, Industrial Relations and Employee Choice: The State of the Workplace in the 1990's.* Kalamazoo, Michigan: W.E. Upjohn Institute for Employment Research.

Block, Richard N., and Benjamin W. Wolkinson. 1985. "Delay in the Union Election Campaign Revisited: A Theoretical and Empirical Analysis." In *Advances in Industrial and Labor Relations* Vol. 3, D. Lewin and D. Lipsky, eds. Greenwich, Connecticut: JAI Press, pp. 53–82.

Borjas, George. 1993. "Immigration Policy, National Origin, and Immigrant Skills: A Comparison of Canada and the United States." In *Small Differences that Matter,* David Card and Richard Freeman, eds. Chicago, Illinois: University of Chicago Press, pp. 21–32.

Borjas, George J., and Valerie A. Ramey. 1994. "Time-Series Evidence on the Sources of Trends in Wage Inequality." *American Economic Review* 84(2): 10–16.

Boychuk, Gerard. 1997. "Are Canadian and U.S. Social Assistance Policies Converging?" Canadian-American Public Policy, Orono, Maine, No. 30.

Bradsher, Keith. 1993. "After Vote, Labor Is Bitter But Big Business Is Elated." *The New York Times,* November 18, p. A21.

Brown, Drusilla, Alan V. Deardorff, and Robert M. Stern. 1997. *Trade and Labor Standards,* Discussion Paper No. 394. School of Public Policy, University of Michigan, Ann Arbor.

Bruce, Peter G. 1989. "Political Parties and Labor Legislation in Canada and the U.S." *Industrial Relations* 28(2): 115–141.

———. 1990. "The Processing of Unfair Labor Practice Cases in the United States and Canada." *Relations Industrielles, Industrial Relations* 45(Spring): 481–511.

Brudney, James J. 1996. "A Famous Victory: Collective Bargaining Protections and the Statutory Aging Process." *North Carolina Law Review* 74(2): 938–1036.

Bureau of National Affairs. 1994. *Individual Employment Rights Reference Manual,* 505, March.

Bureau of National Affairs Labor Relations Reporter: Labor Relations Expediter. 1995a. *Fair Labor Standards Act.* Bureau of National Affairs, Inc., Washington, D.C.

Bureau of National Affairs State Policy and Practice Series, Part 2. 1995b. *State Laws.* Bureau of National Affairs, Inc., Washington, D.C.

Bureau of National Affairs Labor Relations Reporter: Wage and Hour Manual. 1995c. *Fair Labor Standards Act.* Bureau of National Affairs, Inc., Washington, D.C.

Burton, John F., Jr. 1989. "Workers' Compensation in Canada and the United States: Decentralized Approaches and Divergent Outcomes." *John Burton's Workers' Compensation Monitor* (January): 7–12.

Burton, John F., Jr., and Timothy Schmidle. 1996. *1996 Workers' Compensation Yearbook*. Horsham, Pennsylvania: LRP Publications.

Caire, Guy. 1994. "Labour Standards and International Trade." In *International Labour Standards and Economic Interdependence*. Geneva, Switzerland: International Institute for Labour Studies, pp. 297–317.

Canada, Government of. 1988. *Canada Labour Code,* R.S., 1985,C.L-2, December.

———. 1993. *Canada Labour Code*, R.S.Q., 1985,C.27, March.

———. 1995. *A 21st Century Employment System for Canada: Employment Insurance Legislation Highlights*, Ottawa.

Canada Labour Relations Board. 1991. *Annual Report, 1990–91*. Ottawa: Canada Labour Relations Board.

CANSIM. 1998. "Population by Age Sex." Accessed at: <http://www.StatCan.CA/english/pgdb/other/lfs/lfscansim.htm>.

Card, David, and Richard Freeman. 1993. "Small Differences that Matter: Canada vs. the United States." In *Working Under Different Rules,* R. Freeman, ed. New York: Russell Sage Foundation, pp. 189–221.

Card, David, Francis Kramarz, and Thomas Lemieux. 1996. "Changes in the Relative Structure of Wages and Employment: A Comparison of the United States, Canada, and France." Working Paper no. 5487. Cambridge, Massachusetts: National Bureau of Economic Research, March.

Carmichael, Lorne. 1989. "Self-Enforcing Contracts, Shirking, and Life-Cycle Incentives." *Journal of Economic Perspectives* 3(4): 65–84.

Carrothers, A.W.R. 1986. *Collective Bargaining Law in Canada,* 2nd Ed., Toronto, Butterworths.

Charnovitz, Steve. 1987. "The Influence of International Labour Standards on the World Trading Regime." *International Labor Review* 126(4): 565–584.

Christofides, Louis N., Thanasis Stengos, and Robert Swidinsky. 1997. "Welfare Participation and Labour Market Behaviour in Canada." *Canadian Journal of Economics* 30(3): 595–621.

Commerce Clearinghouse Inc. Various years. *Canadian Employment Safety and Health Guide*, each province.

Compa, Lance. 1993. "Labor Rights and Labor Standards in International Trade." *Law & Policy in International Business* 25(1): 165–191.

Cooke, William N. 1985. *Union Organizing and Public Policy; Failure to Secure First Contracts*. Kalamazoo, Michigan: W.E. Upjohn Institute for Employment Research.

————. 1997, "The Influence of Industrial Relations Factors on U.S. Direct Foreign Investment Abroad." *Industrial and Labor Relations Review* 51(1): 3–17.

Crowley, Donald W. 1987. "Judicial Review of Administrative Agencies." *Western Political Quarterly* 40(2): 265–283.

Currie, Janet, and Sheena McConnell. 1991. "The Effect of the Legal Structure of Collective Bargaining on Dispute Costs and Wages." *American Economic Review* 81(4): 693–718.

————. 1996. "Collective Bargaining in the Public Sector: Reply." *American Economic Review* 81(4): 327–328.

Devadason, Evelyn Shymala, and Dunston Ayadurai. 1997. "A Case Study of Malaysia." In *International Trade, Investment and Competitiveness— Trade Union Strategies in a Global Economy.* International Confederation of Free Trade Unions, pp. 261–337.

de Waart, Paul. 1996. "Minimum Labour Standards in International Trade from a Legal Perspective." *Challenges to the New World Trade Organization*, Pitou van Dijck and Gerrit Faber, eds. The Hague/London/Boston: Kluwer Law International, pp. 245–264.

Dinardo, John, and Thomas Lemieux. 1997. "Diverging Male Wage Inequality in the United States and Canada, 1981–1988: Do Institutions Explain the Difference?" *Industrial and Labor Relations Review* 50(4): 629–651.

Doern, G. Bruce, and Brian W. Tomlin. 1991. *Faith and Fear: The Free Trade Story.* Toronto: Stoddart Publishing Co.

Dorsey, Stuart, and Norman Walzer. 1993. "Workers' Compensation, Job Hazards, and Wages." *Industrial and Labor Relations Review* 36(4): 642–654.

Edgren, Gus. 1979. "Fair Labour Standards and Trade Liberalization." *International Labour Review* 118(5): 523–535.

Edwards, Sebastian. 1997. "Trade Policy, Growth, and Income Distribution." *AEA Papers and Proceedings* May: 205–210.

Emmerij, Louis. 1994. "Contemporary Challenges for Labour Standards Resulting from Globalization." In *International Labour Standards and Economic Interdependence.* Geneva, Switzerland: International Institute for Labour Studies, pp. 319–328.

European Union. 1994. "Council Directive 94/45/EC of 22 September 1994 on the Establishment of European Works Councils or a Procedure in Community-Scale Undertakings and Community Scale Groups of Undertakings for the Purposes of Informing and Consulting Employees." Official Journal of the European Communities, L 254, Vol. 37, 30 September, pp. 64–71. Accessed at: <http://europa.eu.int/eur-lex/en/lif/dat/1994/en_394L0045.html>.

————. 1998a. "Council Directive 97/80/EC of 15 December 1997 on the Burden of Proof in Cases of Discrimination Based on Sex." *Official Journal of the European Communities* L 14, Vol. 41, 20 January, pp. 6–8. Accessed at: <http://europa.eu.int/eur-lex/en/lif/dat/1994/en_394L0045.html>.

————. 1998b. "Council Directive 97/81/EC of 15 December 1997 Concerning the Framework Agreement on Part-Time Work concluded by UNICE, CEEP and ETUC." *Official Journal of the European Communities* L 14, Vol. 41, 20 January, pp. 9–14. Accessed at: <http://europa.eu.int/eur-lex/en/lif/dat/1997/en_397L0081.html>.

————. 1998c. "Introduction: The Protocol on Social Policy and the Annexed Agreement," at European Union Internet resources. Accessed at: <http://www.lib.berkeley.edu/GSSI/eu.html> linked to <http://europa.eu.int/comm/sg/scadplus/leg/en/cha/c10110.htm>.

Faragher v. City of Boca Raton, U.S. Supreme Court, 97-282 (1998).

Farnsworth, Clyde. 1993. "Canadian Liberal's Election Could Spell Trouble for NAFTA." *The Fort-Worth Star Telegram*, October 24, p. 24.

Fields, Gary. 1995. *Trade and Labour Standards: A Review of the Issues.* Paris: Organization for Economic Cooperation and Development.

Freeman, Richard. 1994. "A Hard-Headed Look at Labour Standards." In *International Labour Standards and Economic Interdependence,* W. Sengenberger and D. Campbell, eds. Geneva: International Institute for Labour Standards, p. 79–92.

French, John. 1994. "The Declaration of Philadelphia and the Global Social Charter of the United Nations, 1944–45." In *International Labour Standards and Economic Interdependence,* W. Sengenberger and D. Campbell, eds. Geneva: International Institute for Labour Standards, p. 19–26.

Gaston, Noel, and Daniel Trefler. 1994. "Protection, Trade, and Wages: Evidence from U.S. Manufacturing." *Industrial and Labor Relations Review* 47(4): 574–593.

Greenhouse, Steven. 1997. "Apparel Industry Group Moves to End Sweatshops." *New York Times,* April 9, p. 14.

Golub, Stephen S. 1997. "International Labor Standards and International Trade." International Monetary Fund Working Paper 97/37, April.

Gottschalk, Peter, and Robert Moffitt. 1994. "The Growth of Earnings Instability in the US Labor Market." *Brookings Papers on Microeconomic Activity* (2): 217–272.

Groshen, Erica, and Alan B. Krueger. 1990. "The Structure of Supervision and Pay in Hospitals." *Industrial and Labor Relations Review* 43(3): 134s–146s.

Gunderson, Morley. 1998. "Harmonization of Labour Policies Under Trade Liberalization." *Relations Industrielles\ Industrial Relations* 53(1): 24–53.

Gunderson, Morley, Robert Hebdon, and Douglas Hyatt. 1996. "Collective Bargaining in the Public Sector: Comment." *American Economic Review* 86(1): 315–326.

Hansson, Gote. 1983. *Social Clauses and International Trade: An Economic Analysis of Labour Standards in Trade Policy.* London and Canberra: Croon Helm/New York: St. Martin's Press.

Harcourt, Tim. 1997. "A Case Study of Australia." In *International Trade, Investment and Competitiveness–Trade Union Strategies in a Global Economy,* International Confederation of Free Trade Unions, pp.1–67.

Hardin, Patrick. 1990 and updates. *The Developing Labor Law,* Third edition. Washington, D.C.: Bureau of National Affairs.

Harris v. Forklift Systems. 1993. U.S. Supreme Court, No. 92-1168, 63 FEP Cases 225.

Health Canada, Health System and Policy Division. 1998. "Canada's Health System." Accessed at: <http://www.hc_sc.gc.ca/datapcb/datahesa/hlthsys/Ehlthsys.htm>.

Health Care and Retirement Systems v. NLRB. 1994. 511 U.S. 571.

Hirsch, Barry. 1992. "Firm Investment Behavior and Collective Bargaining Strategy." *Industrial Relations* 31(Winter): 95–121.

Hoge, Warren. 1997. "Britons Back Labor Party; Conservatives Are Routed after 18 Years of Control." *The New York Times,* May 2, Sec. A, p. 1.

Hufbauer, Gary, and Jeffrey Schott. 1992. *Western Hemisphere Economic Integration.* Washington, D.C.: Institute for International Economics.

Human Resources Development Canada (HRDC). 1995a. *Employment Standards Legislation in Canada,* 1995–96 Edition. Ottawa, Canada.

———. 1995b. *Information on Labour Standards,* Chapter 8, Ottawa, Canada.

———. 1995c. *Information on Labour Standards,* Chapter 10, Ottawa, Canada.

———. 1997. New Employment Insurance System. Accessed at: <http://www.hrdc-drhc.gc.ca/hrdc/ei/ina068_e.html>.

———. 1998a. "Canada Pension Plan." Accessed at: <http://www.hrdc_drhc.gc.ca/isp/cpp/cppind_e.shtml>.

———. 1998b. "Overview of the Old Age Security Program." Accessed at: <http://www.hrdc_drhc.gc.ca/isp/oas/oasind_e.shtml>.

Hyatt, Doug, and Boris Kralj. 1992. "Workers' Compensation Costs and Competitiveness: Issues and Inter-Jurisdictional Comparisons." In Women and Industrial Relations, D. Carter, ed. Kingston, Ontario: Queen's University, pp. 421–430.

International Confederation of Free Trade Unions–ICFTU. 1996. "Congress Resolutions." *Sixteenth World Congress of the ICFTU, Brussels, June 25–29, 1996.* Accessed at: <http://www.icftu.org>.

International Labor Organization–ILO. 1995. *Lists of Ratifications by Convention and by Country (as of 31 December, 1994).* International Labour Conference, 82nd Session, Report III, Part 5.

Jain, Hem. 1992. "Wrongful Dismissals in Non-Union Companies in North America." In *Women and Industrial Relations,* D. Carter, ed. Kingston, Ontario: Queen's University, pp. 195–202.

Jennings, Thomas F., Joanne Guth, W. Scott Baker, Magdolna Kornis, Walker Pollard, and Hugh Arce. 1997. *Caribbean Basin Economic Recovery Act: Impact on the United States,* Twelfth Report 1996, Investigation No. 332-227. United States International Trade Commission Publication 3058, September. Accessed at: <http://www.usitc.gov:80/wais/reports/arc/W3058.HTM>.

Johnson, George. 1998. "Changes in Earnings Inequality: The Role of Demand Shifts." *Journal of Economic Perspectives* 12(2): 101–116.

Kahn, Joseph, and David Sanger. 1999. "Impasse on Trade Delivers a Stinging Blow to Clinton." *New York Times,* Dec 5, p. 1.1.

Karier, Thomas. 1991. "Unions and the U.S. Comparative Advantage." *Industrial Relations* 30(1): 1–19.

———. 1992. "Trade Deficits and Labor Unions: Myths and Realities." In *Unions and Economic Competitiveness,* Lawrence Mishel and Paula B. Voos, eds. Armonk, New York: Sharpe Publishing, pp. 15–39.

———. 1995. "U.S. Foreign Production and Unions." *Industrial Relations* 34(2): 107–117.

Kelly, John G. 1991. *Human Resource Management and the Human Rights Process,* 2nd Ed., Don Mills, Ontario: CCH Canada Ltd.

Keil, Manfred, and Louis Pantuosco. 1998. "Canadian and U.S. Unemployment Rates: A Comparison Based on Regional Data." *Canadian Public Policy* 24, supplement, S38–S55.

Kochan, Thomas A., and Richard N. Block. 1977. "An Interindustry Analysis of Bargaining Outcomes: Preliminary Evidence from Two-Digit Industries." *Quarterly Journal of Economics* 91(3): 431–452.

Krueger, Alan B. 1991. "The Evolution of Unjust Dismissal Legislation in the United States." *Industrial and Labor Relations Review* 44(4): 644–660.

Krugman, Paul R. 1994. *Rethinking International Trade.* Cambridge, Massachusetts: M.I.T. Press.

Kruse, Douglas L. 1988. "International Trade and the Labor Market Experience of Displaced Workers." *Industrial and Labor Relations Review* 41(3): 402–416.

Kumar, Pradeep. 1991. *Canadian Labour Relations: An Information Manual.* Kingston, Ontario: Industrial Relations Centre, Queens University.

Lang, Kevin, and Jay Zagorsky. 1998. "Why Are Canadian and U.S. Unemployment Rates So Highly Correlated?" *Canadian Public Policy* 24(supplement): S56–S71.

Langille, Brian. 1991. "Canadian Labour Law Reform and Free Trade." *Ottawa Law Reform* 21(3): 583–622.

————. 1994. "Labour Standards in the Globalized Economy and the Free Trade/Fair Trade Debate." In *International Labour Standards and Economic Interdependence.* Geneva, Switzerland: International Institute for Labour Studies, pp. 329–338.

Lee, Eddy. 1997. "Globalization and Labour Standards: A Review of Issues." *International Labour Review* 136(2): 173–189.

Levitt, Howard. 1985. *The Law of Dismissal in Canada.* Aurora, Ontario: Canada Law Books, Inc.

Lipset, Seymour Martin. 1989. *Continental Divide: The Values and Institutions of the United States and Canada.* Toronto and Washington, D.C.: D.C. Howe Institute and National Planning Association.

Lyon, Peyton. 1987. "CUFTA and Canadian Independence." In *Canadian-American Free Trade: Historical, Political, and Economic Dimensions*, A.R. Riggs and Tom Velk, eds. Halifax, Nova Scotia: The Institute for Research on Public Policy.

Mahant, Edelgard E. 1993. *Free Trade in American-Canadian Relations.* Malabar, Florida: Krieger Publishing Co.

Maier, Heribert. 1994. "International Labor Standards and Economic Integration: The Perspective of the International Labor Organization." In *International Labor Standards and Global Integration: The Proceedings of a Symposium.* U.S. Department of Labor, pp. 9–14.

Marshall, Ray. 1994. "The Importance of International Labor Standards in a More Competitive Global Economy." In *International Labour Standards and Economic Interdependence,* Werner Sengenberger and Duncan Campbell, eds. Geneva: International Institute for Labor Standards, pp. 65–78.

Martin, Richard. 1991. "Evaluating Free Trade: A Perspective from the CLC." *The Economic Impact and Implications of the Canada-U.S. Free Trade Agreement,* Fakhari Siddiqui, ed. Lewiston, New York and Queenston, Ontario: The Edwin Mellon Press, pp. 25–36.

Mendenhall, William, Robert Shaeffer, and Dennis Wackerly. 1986. *Mathematical Statistics With Applications,* 3rd. Ed. Boston, Massachusetts: Duxbury.

Meritor Savings Bank v. Vinson. 1986. 477 U.S. 57.

Mitchell, Alison. 1997. "Clinton Clears First Hurdle on Fast Track Trade Legislation." *The New York Times*, November 4.

Morissette, Rene, John Myles, and Garnett Picot. 1995. "Earnings Polarization in Canada, 1969–1991." In *Labour Market Polarization and Social Policy Reform*, Keith G. Banting and Charles M. Beach, eds. Kingston, Ontario: School of Policy Studies, Queen's University, pp. 23–50.

Mullan, David. 1993. "Judicial Deference to Executive Decision-Making: Evolving Concepts of Responsibility." *Queen's Law Journal* 19(1): 137–178.

Murphy, Kevin M., W. Craig Riddell, and Paul M. Romer. 1998. "Wages, Skills, and Technology in the United States and Canada." In *General Purpose Technologies and Economic Growth*, Tlhanan Helpman, ed. Cambridge, Massachusetts: The MIT Press, pp. 283–309.

NLRB v. Bell Aerospace. 1974. 416 U.S. 267.

NLRB v. Kentucky River Community Care Inc. 2001. U.S. Supreme Court, No. 99-1815. Accessed at: <http://www.findlaw.com/casecode/supreme.html>, party name search = "Kentucky River."

Nickell, Steven. 1997. "Unemployment and Labor Market Rigidities: Europe versus North America." *Journal of Economic Perspectives* 11(3): 55–74.

North American Agreement on Labor Cooperation. 1993. Between the Government of the United States of America, the Government of Canada, and the Government of the United Mexican States, September 13 at Internet address <http://www.usitc.gov:80/wais/reports/arc/W3058.htm>.

Novak, Rita M., and Douglas K. Somerlot. 1990. *Delay on Appeal: A Process for Identifying Causes and Cures*. Chicago, Illinois: American Bar Association.

Odgers, Cameron, and Julian Betts. 1997. "Do Unions Reduce Investment? Evidence from Canada." *Industrial and Labor Relations Review* 51(1): 18–36.

Organization for Economic Cooperation and Development (OECD). 1996. *Trade, Employment and Labour Standards: A Study of Core Workers' Rights and International Trade*. Geneva, Switzerland: International Institute for Labour Studies.

Piore, Michael. 1990. "Labor Standards and Business Strategies." In *Labor Standards and Development in the Global Economy*, S. Herzenberg and J. Perez-Lopez, eds. Washington, D.C.: U.S. Department of Labor (Bureau of International Labor Affairs), pp. 35–49.

Report and Recommendations of the Commission on the Future of Workers-Management Relations. 1994, December.

Richardson, David. 1995. "Income Inequality and Trade: How to Think, What to Conclude." *Journal of Economic Perspectives* 9(3): 33–55.

Richardson, David H. 1997. "Changes in the Distribution of Wages in Canada, 1981–1992." *Canadian Journal of Economics* 30(3): 622–643.

Riddell, W. Craig, and Andrew Sharpe. 1998. "The Canada-U.S. Unemployment Gap: An Introduction and Overview," *Canadian Public Policy* 24(supplement): S1-S37.

Roberts, Karen, and Michael Madden. 1992. "Workers' Compensation as an Economic Development Issue." In *Women and Industrial Relations*, D. Carter, ed. Kingston, Ontario: Queen's University, pp. 409–420.

Roberts, Karen, and Philip Smith. 1992. "The Effect of Labor Cost Differences on the Location of Economic Activity under the U.S.-Canada Free Trade Agreement." *Economic Development Quarterly* 6(1): 52–63.

Rodrick, Dani. 1994. "Labor Standards in International Trade: Do They Matter and What Do We Do About Them?" *Overseas Development Council, Policy Essay No. 20,* pp. 35–79.

Rugman, Alan. 1991. "Adjustments by Multinational Firms to Free Trade." In *Economic Opportunities in Freer U.S. Trade with Canada,* F. Menz and S. Stevens, eds. Albany, New York: State University of New York Press, pp. 53–66.

Schneid, Thomas. 1992. *The Americans with Disabilities Act.* New York: Van Nostrand Reinhold.

Schnell, John F., and Cynthia Gramm. 1996. "The Empirical Relationship Between Employers' Strike Replacement Strategy and Strike Duration." *Industrial and Labor Relations Review* 47(6): 189–206.

Servais, J.M. 1989. "The Social Clause in Trade Agreements: Wishful Thinking or an Instrument of Social Progress." *International Labour Review* 128(4): 423–432.

Sharma, Basu, and Anthony Giles. 1994. "Effects of the Wage-Effort Bargain and Social Labor Policies on Competitiveness: A Ten Country Study." In *Proceedings of the XXXth Conference,* Esther Deom and Anthony E. Smith, eds. Canadian Industrial Relations Association, pp. 249–260.

Slaughter, Matthew J. 1997. "Per Capita Income Convergence and the Role of International Trade." *American Economic Review* 87(2): 194–199.

Smith, Murray. 1988. "The Free Trade Agreement in Context." In *The Canada-United States Free Trade Agreement: The Global Impact,* J. Schott and M. Smith, eds. Washington, D.C.: Institute for International Economics, pp. 37–64.

Sockell, Donna. 1986. "The Scope of Mandatory Bargaining: A Critique and Proposal." *Industrial and Labor Relations Review* 40(1): 19–34.

Springer, Beverly. 1994. *The European Union and Its Citizens: The Social Agenda.* Westport, Conn. and London: Greenwood Press.

Srinivasan, T.N. 1995. "International Trade and Labour Standards from an Economic Perspective." In *Challenges to the New World Trade Organization,* Pitou van Dijck and Gerrit Faber, eds. The Hague/London/Boston: Kluwer Law International, pp. 239–243.

———. 1997. "The Common External Tariff of a Customs Union." *Japan and the World Economy* 9(4): 447.

———. 1998. "Trade and Human Rights." In *Representation of Constituent Interests in the Design and Implementation of U.S. Trade Policies,* Alan Deardorff and Robert Stern, eds. Ann Arbor, Michigan: University of Michigan Press.

St. Antoine, Theodore. 1988. "At-Will Employment: An Overview." Memorandum Prepared for the Section of Labor and Employment Law of the American Bar Association, 9.

Stamps, James E., Magdolna Kornis, and James Tsao. 1996. *Caribbean Basin Economic Recovery Act: Impact on U.S. Consumers and Taxpayers.* Eleventh Report 1995, Investigation No. 332-227, United States International Trade Commission Publication 2994, September. Accessed at: <http://www.usitc.gov:80/wais/reports/arc/W2994.HTM>.

Statistics Canada. 1998. *Average Weekly Hours, For Employees Paid by the Hour,* 72F0002_XDE. Accessed at: <http://www.statcan.ca:80/english/Pgdb/People/labour.htm>.

Stieber, Jack, and Richard N. Block. 1992. "Comment on Alan B. Krueger, 'The Evolution of Unjust Dismissal Legislation in the United States.'" *Industrial and Labor Relations Review* 45(4): 792–796.

Swinnerton, Kenneth, and Gregory Schoepfle. 1994. "Labor Standards in the Context of a Global Economy." *Monthly Labor Review* 117(9): 52–59.

Tille, Cedric. 1998. "Decomposition of the Unemployment Gap between Canada and the United States: Duration or Incidence." *Canadian Public Policy* 24(supplement): S90–S102.

Topel, Robert. 1997. "Factor Proportions and Relative Wages: The Supply Side Determinants of Wage Inequality." *Journal of Economic Perspectives* 11(2): 55–74.

Treaty of Versailles. 1919. Part XIII, Labour, Section 1. Accessed at: <http://history.acusd.edu/gen/text/versaillestreaty/ver387.html>.

U.S. Chamber of Commerce. 1995. *Analysis of Workers' Compensation Laws, 1955.* Washington, D.C.

———. 1996. *1996 Analysis of Workers' Compensation Laws.* Washington, D.C.

U.S. Department of Commerce. 1998a. *Statistical Abstract of the United States, 1.* Accessed at: <http://www.census.gov/statab/www/>.

———. 1998b. *Statistical Abstract of the United States,* Table 7, p. 10. Accessed at: <http://www.census.gov/prod/2001pubs/statab/sec01.pdf>.

———. 1998c. *Statistical Abstract of the United States.* Table 13, p.14. Accessed at: <http://www.census.gov/prod/2001pubs/statab/sec01.pdf_>.

———. 1998d. *Statistical Abstract of the United States.* Table 251, p. 158. Accessed at: <http://www.census.gov/prod/2001pubs/statab/sec04.pdf>.

———. 1998e. *Statistical Abstract of the United States.* Table 684, p.428. Accessed at: <http://www.census.gov/prod/2001pubs/statab/sec13.pdf>.

U.S. Department of Labor. 1994a. "International Comparisons of Manufacturing Hourly Compensation Costs, 1993." *News: United States Department of Labor, Bureau of Labor Statistics,* USDL-94-261, May 24.

———. 1994b. *ETA Handbook,* No. 394. Washington, DC: Unemployment Insurance Service.

———. 1997. *State Workers' Compensation Laws.* Washington, D.C.: Employment and Standards Administration, January.

———. 1998. *National Employment, Hours and Earnings: Average Weekly Hours of Production Workers,* Series ID: EES00510005, Bureau of Labor Statistics. Accessed at: <http://146.142.4.24/ cgi_bin/surveymost>.

———. 2001. *Minimum Wage and Overtime Hours Under the Fair Labor Standards Act,* Employment Standards Administration, Wage and Hour Division. Accessed at: <http://www.dol.gov/dol/esa/public/regs/statutes/whd/page_br.htm>, January.

van Liemt, Gjisbert. 1989. "Minimum Labour Standards and International Trade: Would a Social Clause Work?" *Intenational Labour Review* 128(4): 433–448.

Weil, David. 1995. "Mandating Health and Safety Committees: Lessons from the United States." In *Proceedings of the 47thAnnual Meeting of the Industrial Relations Research Association, Washington, D.C., January 6–8, 1995,* Paula Voos, ed. Madison, Wisconsin: Industrial Relations Research Association, pp. 273–281.

Weiler, Paul C. 1983. "Promises to Keep: Securing Workers' Rights to Self-Organization Under the NLRA." *Harvard Law Review* 96: 1769–1827.

White, Randall. 1988. *Fur Trade to Free Trade: Putting the Canada-U.S. Free Trade Agreement in Historical Context.* Toronto and Oxford: Dundern Press.

Wolkinson, Benjamin, and Richard N. Block. 1996. *Employment Discrimination: The Workplace Rights of Employees and Employers.* Cambridge, Massachusetts, USA and Oxford, UK: Blackwell Publishers.

Wood, Adrian. 1995. "How Trade Hurt Unskilled Workers." *Journal of Economic Perspectives* 9: 57–80.

World Trade Organization. 1996. "Singapore Ministerial Declaration."
    December 13, 1996. World Trade Organization Ministerial Conference,
    Singapore, 9–13 December. Accessed at: <http:// www.wto.org/wto/
    Whats_new/wtodec.htm>.
World Trade Organization. 1998. "About the WTO—Labor Standards: Not
    on the Agenda." Accessed at: <http://www.wto.org/about/beyond7.htm>.

The Authors

Richard Norman Block is a professor in the School of Labor and Industrial Relations at Michigan State University. He is the author of numerous articles and books on such issues as collective bargaining, labor and employment law, the relationship between law and practice and industrial relations, industrial relations and structural economic change, employee privacy, international labor standards, and government sponsored employee training. His work has appeared in all major journals in the industrial relations field. He has been a visiting faculty member at Columbia University, the University of Toronto, and the London School of Economics and Political Science. He is an experienced labor management neutral, listed on all major panels, including several private panels.

Karen Roberts is a professor in the School of Labor and Industrial Relations at Michigan State University. She is an active researcher on issues related to international labor standards, with a special emphasis on workers' compensation. Her research on these topics has been published in *Industrial Relations*, *Relations Industrielles*, the *Labor Law Journal*, and the *Economic Development Quarterly*.

R. Oliver Clarke served as Principal Administrator of the Social Affairs and Industrial Relations Division of the Organization for Economic Cooperation and Development (OECD) in Paris from 1970 to 1988. Through this position, he became an expert in comparative industrial relations systems, and all aspects of labor market policy. He is the author of numerous publications on international labor issues. After retiring from the OECD in 1988, Mr. Clarke was a visiting faculty member at the University of Western Australia, Curtin University (Australia), University of New South Wales, University of Leuven (Belgium), Michigan State University, the University of British Columbia, the American Graduate School of International Management (Arizona), and the Chinese Culture University (Taiwan). Mr. Clarke passed away in August, 2001.

Index

The italic letters *f*, *n*, and *t* following a page number indicate that the subject information is within a figure, note, or table, respectively, on that page.

About the Institute

The W.E. Upjohn Institute for Employment Research is a nonprofit research organization devoted to finding and promoting solutions to employment-related problems at the national, state, and local levels. It is an activity of the W.E. Upjohn Unemployment Trustee Corporation, which was established in 1932 to administer a fund set aside by the late Dr. W.E. Upjohn, founder of The Upjohn Company, to seek ways to counteract the loss of employment income during economic downturns.

The Institute is funded largely by income from the W.E. Upjohn Unemployment Trust, supplemented by outside grants, contracts, and sales of publications. Activities of the Institute comprise the following elements: 1) a research program conducted by a resident staff of professional social scientists; 2) a competitive grant program, which expands and complements the internal research program by providing financial support to researchers outside the Institute; 3) a publications program, which provides the major vehicle for disseminating the research of staff and grantees, as well as other selected works in the field; and 4) an Employment Management Services division, which manages most of the publicly funded employment and training programs in the local area.

The broad objectives of the Institute's research, grant, and publication programs are to 1) promote scholarship and experimentation on issues of public and private employment and unemployment policy, and 2) make knowledge and scholarship relevant and useful to policymakers in their pursuit of solutions to employment and unemployment problems.

Current areas of concentration for these programs include causes, consequences, and measures to alleviate unemployment; social insurance and income maintenance programs; compensation; workforce quality; work arrangements; family labor issues; labor-management relations; and regional economic development and local labor markets.